Supply Chain Visibility

Dedicated to Dr Kitty Dickerson and Maxine Clark

Supply Chain Visibility

From Theory to Practice

JONAH SAINT MCINTIRE

Routledge
Taylor & Francis Group

LONDON AND NEW YORK

First published in paperback 2024

First published 2014 by Gowar Publishing

Published 2016 by Routledge
4 Park Square, Milton Park, Abingdon, Oxon OX14 4RN

and by Routledge
605 Third Avenue, New York, NY 10158

Routledge is an imprint of the Taylor & Francis Group, an informa business

Publisher's Note
The publisher has gone to great lengths to ensure the quality of this reprint but points out that some imperfections in the original copies may be apparent.

British Library Cataloguing in Publication Data
A catalogue record for this book is available from the British Library.

Library of Congress Cataloging-in-Publication Data
LoC data has been applied for.

ISBN: 978-1-4724-1346-8 (hbk)
ISBN: 978-1-03-283702-4 (pbk)
ISBN: 978-1-315-61134-1 (ebk)

DOI: 10.4324/9781315611341

Contents

List of Figures

List of Tables

About the Author

Jonah McIntire conceived and developed the framework proposed in this book after years of deep focus on the subject of supply chain visibility and realizing that newcomers to the field were at a disadvantage due to the low volume and uncoordinated nature of the published work on the topic. Jonah is co-founder of Clear Abacus, a cloud-computing transport planning and optimization solution, a company combining cutting edge computing and supply chain expertise. Prior to founding Clear Abacus his career in the supply chain field spans consulting, product management, change management, supply chain information systems, process re-engineering, and outsourcing. He has a broad global perspective, having lived or executed major supply chain projects in the last ten years in Denmark, France, the UK, Japan, China, Singapore, Switzerland, the USA, and Canada. In the area of supply chain visibility, Jonah's work experience includes system selection and deployment for a major retailer, solution and integration consulting as a software vendor, IT product management for a logistics service provider, and periodic publications, presentations, and interviews on the subject.

Preface

Business leaders expect supply chain visibility to be impactful. Industry surveys such as the IBM Chief Supply Chain Officer survey of 2010 and the Cap Gemini visibility software study of 2012 show supply chain visibility ranked as a top concern for supply chain executives. Far from a purely academic pursuit, supply chain leaders are approving substantial investments for change initiatives and IT systems on the promise that the supply chain visibility they deliver will improve company financial performance. But for all the interest and market activity, the subject itself remains abstract, with very few detailed studies available as guides for new managers embarking on supply chain visibility initiatives. Readers of this book will value the insights found within because it:

1. Places them in a measurably stronger position within their leadership role when deciding how to leverage visibility solutions; and

2. Walks them past the mine field of ineffective approaches or technologies to the frontiers of proven supply chain visibility value. They can begin their personal involvement in this area by standing on the shoulders of proven best practices, something which is not available yet in the supply chain literature.

In *Supply Chain Visibility: From Theory to Practice*, readers with backgrounds in supply chain management, system integration, strategy consulting, and enterprise software receive a critical primer on the subject. The book has two sections operating on two motifs. In the first section, starting with Chapter 1, the book reviews the research which has been done to date on supply chain visibility, including its history. This helps orientate readers and sets the stage for a novel supply chain visibility framework, explained in Chapter 2. This includes a more useful definitional framework for supply chain visibility, one that empowers business leaders to connect their projects tasks or work streams back to a strategic message about why supply chain visibility is worth the organizational resources. Then a review is made of the prerequisites needed for a successful visibility solution. Finally, a visibility fitness scorecard is suggested, which enables very dissimilar approaches to be compared in terms of their final quality as a visibility solution. In the second section, the book looks at the practical aspects of supply chain visibility solutions. It begins with detailed reviews of the eight most common types of supply chain visibility. For each visibility type a set of discovery questions, or indicators of potential fit, are offered. The second section also addresses the question of how to acquire visibility, particularly visibility technology. It begins with a review of the options available for acquiring visibility technology, including the benefits and risks for each option. Since private development is a major approach to supply chain visibility software, the book also goes into detail with guidance on best-practices for in-house designed systems. In particular, an object-model and key technical suggestions are provided for the types of supply chain visibility discussed. The second section provides key details which would typically only be available to very experienced consultants who have worked in the supply chain visibility solution space across industries and global markets. The book closes with a look at the cutting edge of supply chain visibility technology, and at technologies which exist, although not yet widely adopted, will revolutionize the visibility solution space.

Most readers will have come to this book with purpose, not as a casual interest, because supply chain visibility has come into their professional life and they need to know how to get the most out of it. That is what this book is about. It will bring a supply chain professional as far up to speed as possible without direct work experience in the domain, and leave them prepared to be a savvy participant in critical planning and implementation activities.

Reader Profile

The parent field of supply chain management is itself a specialty, combining many disciplines into a powerful management paradigm for cross-organization flows of material, capital, and information. So anyone reading this book is probably a specialist (i.e. a supply chain specialist). Not only are they likely to be a specialist before picking up this book: it was written with that background in mind. The material that follows would be appropriate for individuals with these kinds of backgrounds:

- A supply chain manager in a company, executing operations or improving business processes.

- An IT professional charged with supporting supply chain activities, especially selecting or building software in support of supply chain management.

- A client-facing staff at a supply chain service provider, such as a 3PL or sourcing agency.

- A consultant providing strategy, technology, or investment advice on supply chain matters.

- A finance professional responsible for supply chain operations and projects.

- A member of a steering committee in a company considering a new supply chain visibility project.

- A risk management professional looking at supply chain risk vectors and mitigation strategies.

- A university student, probably at the end of a MS or MBA program.

- An academic researcher focused on supply chain coordination and control.

- A member of an acquisition or merger team trying to rationalize or consolidate diverging supply chain technology portfolios.

- A logistics manager for a not-for-profit or humanitarian organization.

For those without this kind of background, it's still okay to proceed. But there won't be much in the way of an introduction to supply chain management, its strategies, history, or current trends.

Practitioner vs. Researcher

Throughout the book, I make use of a distinction between the needs of *practitioners* as compared to *researchers*. As context, I am assuming that researchers pursue the creation or verification of knowledge as its own goal. Typically, this would be occurring in an academic setting, but could also be tied to some parts of business such as consulting. Conversely, I assume that practitioners are primarily interested in the output or the work needed to get an output, as some part of their job performance or career is tied to its success. Researchers study and refine visibility; practitioners use visibility to improve their businesses.

Acknowledgments

Now would be a good point to give some appreciative recognition of those who helped achieve this book. First, thanks to the editing team at Gower and particularly to Jonathan Norman who convinced me they were serious about supply chain management topics. I also owe thanks to the small portion of interviewees who were brave enough to go on record for the book: Peter Karel, Shanton Wilcox, Christoph Lienhard, Scott Fenwick, and Graham Wilkie. Their interview transcripts are available in Appendix A. Thanks to my colleagues in the product management team for client-facing IT systems at Panalpina; Christoph Lienhard, Jianzheng Wu, Stefan Gille, and Simon Lutz. Together we had some truly inspirational discussions on the topic of supply chain visibility. Professionally, but further afield, I'd like to thank some specific mentors who helped guide me into supply chain as a domain for my career, or supported my rise within it. Dr Hyunjoo Oh and Dr Kitty Dickerson helped set me on this course, and Maxine Clark made my first significant role in the domain possible. Dennis Sheldon, Mike Early, and Jeff Fulmer were excellent role models during my time at Build-a-Bear Workshop. Marty Levy, Bob Kramer, and Jim Janetzko were fantastic collaborators at UPS. David Landau, Scott Fenwick, Stephen Keefe, Heather Mahan, Eddie Capel, and Pete Sinisgalli were real inspirations and the reason I joined Manhattan Associates. I also wish to say thanks to Michael Heavey, who bridged a generation and cultural gap and provided key mentoring advice for years. And then there are the personal thanks to be given. The first goes to my wife, best friend, and evergreen Geraldine Meier. My immediate family has also been a principle source of encouragement, especially Marsha McIntire and Seth McIntire. Last, thanks to my best friends: Zach Hopkins, Kristen Totleben, Jennifer Benoit-Bryan, Josh Bryan, and Jamie Langbart.

Jonah Saint McIntire
Basel, Switzerland

List of Acronyms

ARA Model	Agent Resource Activity Model
IMP	Industrial Marketing and Purchasing Group
ERP	Enterprise Resource Planning
SMS	Short Message Service
COO	Chief Operations Officer
PDF	Portable Document Format
PO	Purchase Order
ROA	Return on Assets
EVA	Economic Value Add
GM	Gross Margin
WIP	Work in Progress
3PL	Third Party Logistics Provider
WMS	Warehouse Management System
SKU	Stock Keeping Unit
MHU	Material Handling Unit
MBOL	Master Bill of Lading
USB	Universal Serial Bus
SIM	Subscriber Identity Module
RFQ	Request for Quotations
FSM	Finite State Machine
AI	Artificial Intelligence
COTS	Complete Off the Shelf
SaaS	Software as a Service
CRM	Customer Relationship Management
UPS	United Postal Service
RFID	Radio Frequency Identification
ROI	Return on Investment
CIO	Chief Information Officer
EEM	Extended Enterprise Management
FEMA	Federal Emergency Management Agency

LPNs	License Plate Numbers
LSP	Logistics Service Provider
TMS	Transport Management System
SME	Small to Medium Sized Enterprise
UI	User Interface
GUI	Graphic User Interface
EDI	Electronic Data Interchange
ASN	Advanced Shipping Notice
UMHU	Unique Material Handling Unit
SQL	Structured Query Language
ACID	Atomicity, Consistency, Isolation, Durability
ATP	Available to Promise
DC	Distribution Center
IT	Information Technology
4PL	Fourth Party Logistics Provider
GPS	Geospatial Positioning System

PART 1
Supply Chain Visibility in Theory

The History and Definition of Supply Chain Visibility

The Origins of Supply Chain Visibility

Supply chain visibility has broad multidisciplinary roots, much like its parent field supply chain management. The theoretical basis and supporting academic research on supply chain visibility is therefore wider than it is deep. Supply chain visibility, at its earliest stage of usage, was simply the notion that information about the global supply chain would lead to better local supply chain decisions, a notion so basic it's practically at the core of supply chain management itself (Storey and Emberson, 2001). Classic supply chain failures such as the Forrester (or "bullwhip") effect derive directly from the lack of global information when making local decisions such as production or inventory level setting (Lee, Padmanabhan, and Whang, 1997).

Theoretical models from the 1990s, such as the A–R–A model (later called the IMP model after the "Industrial Marketing and Purchasing Group" which sponsored its development) of industrial networks research (Baig and Khan, 2001; Mathews and Shulman, 1999) also included access to global information on the supply chain as a major driver for improved outcomes. In the A–R–A model (so named because it treats the supply chain as a set of "Agents Resources and Activities") there is an explicit link between game theory concepts of the agent (or firm's) information set and its best strategy. Because each firm (or agent) in the supply chain has different information, even if they all behave fully rationally their behaviors will appear unaligned and perhaps contradictory. One strategy for improved performance of individual firms in this supply chain theoretical model is for them to acquire broader information, hence, to enact supply chain visibility. The figure on the following page is a representation of the IMP network model adapted from Mathews and Shulman (1999).

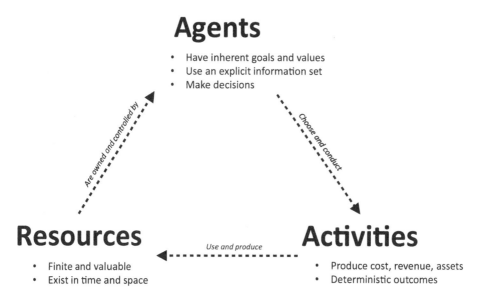

Figure 1.1   The IMP network model

The 1990s was also a period when two trends came together to focus the supply chain researcher community on the potential for visibility: EDI and the consumer internet. The overarching theme in these years was that supply chain information contained significant competitive advantages for those who could harness them. These were a mix of advantages in efficiency (lower inventory, lower transport costs, reduced labor, reduced wastage, etc.) as well as effectiveness (product design, pricing, and strategic supplier selection). In 1989 a well-regarded paper suggested that there was a direct and inverse correlation between *informational* resources needed to maintain a given service level and the enterprise-wide *inventory* level (Dudley and Lasserre, 1989). Hence in the 1990s the phrase "information instead of inventory" grew in popularity, appearing in formal journal articles, then working papers and presentations, and finally in practitioner journals (Bytheway, 1995). Likewise important improvements in barcoding and EDI lead to significant new potential for information exchange and coordination in the supply chains of apparel (Cooper, 2006) and food products (Hill and Scudder, 2001). This academic interest was paralleled by practitioner interest and actions. By 2003, EDI adoption rates among the most competitive companies (the Fortune 100) was over 90 percent while the rest of the companies surveyed were adopting at a dismal 3 percent rate (Shaw, 2003 as described by Salo and Karjaluoto, 2006).

Supply chain theoretical models in the 2000s seem to take for granted that supply chains exist across organizational boundaries, i.e. that a supply chain is de facto made up of multiple independent companies (McAdam and McCormack, 2001), and that the inclusion and role of the individual companies was derived from their specializations (Picot, Reichwald, and Wigand, 2003). The research and practitioner shift was towards hybrid organizational structures (Picot, Reichwald, and Wigand, 2003), also called hollow enterprises (McIntire, 2010), where the supply chain members are dependent on each other for survival because their individual organization no longer has the resources to complete its market function alone. The models promulgated in the 2000s specifically included the sharing of information as a key driver for the creation and success of the supply chain network (Albani, Müssigman, and Zaha, 2007). The key difference between earlier works from the 1990s, such as the IMP network model, is that models from the 2000s tended to view supply chains as strategic enablers or hindrances rather than operational factors to be rendered more efficient. A core part of the strategic value of a supply chain was how it did or could handle information flows and increase the situational awareness and thus competitive power of the participating firms. This trend was occurring in supply chain research, but also in the context of globalization which was driving serious re-thinking about what the basis and boundaries of an organization should be. Pivotal articles such as "The core competence of the corporation (Prahalad and Hamel, 1990)" were focusing attention on the need to specialize in terms of capability, not just market position. Also of interest in the 2000s was the extent to which virtual markets, e-commerce portals, and similar arrangements could overtake physical supply chain value-adding steps (Rayport and Sviokla, 1995). Again, the assumption here was that greater information access and situational awareness would drive stronger supply chains.

So it's safe to say that supply chain management theory has posited that improved information access is an important goal since at least the 1980s, effectively coincidental with the founding of the field itself. Although theoretical models used to understand and improve supply chains have changed, none have deviated in the belief that there exists a correlation between greater situational awareness and greater supply chain performance. Knowledge is power, so to speak. What this says is that supply chain management has always appreciated *having* visibility, i.e. having more information and greater situational awareness. That is subtly different from *pursuing* supply chain visibility as a concept, technique, process, or goal. When did the supply chain academic community begin talking about supply chain visibility as something to be done, rather than a measure of the quality of the supply chain itself? And why did the switch occur?

Unfortunately, it's not clear when academics (or practitioners for that matter) started thinking of supply chain visibility in this way, i.e. as a solution rather than a quality. At least as far back as 1987 there was concern in academic research about how supply chain managers or logistics managers could increase their visibility in to international supply chains (Houlihan, 1987). But there doesn't appear to be a specific agenda of techniques or solutions called "supply chain visibility" which was being proposed to meet that need. It's a subtle difference to think of visibility as a quality vs. visibility as a solution. As an analogy, Henry Ford was supposed to have faced a market where his customers wanted better horses, not automobiles. Only later, when his efforts made the concept of transport synonymous with automobiles, did the consumer sentiment switch in terminology. Something similar happened with the term supply chain visibility, which began as something to measure (like costs) but evolved into a solution to improve overall supply chain or business performance. In the domain of supply chain visibility researchers clearly documented the need for greater visibility before that term came to be used as an agenda or toolset for improving information flow and situational awareness.

A series of industry journals, academic journals, and scholarly textbooks published from the year 2000 onward show discussions of supply chain visibility *as a solution* as opposed to a quality to be measured (Thompson, Manrodt, Holcomb, Allen, and Hoffman, 2000; Joshi, 2000; Reyes, Raisinghani, and Singh, 2002; Simchi-Levi, Kaminsky, and Simchi-Levi, 2003). Sometime before these articles and books came to publication, the supply chain research community had shifted to thinking of supply chain visibility as a *solution to a problem*. This makes intuitive sense given that off the shelf "solutions" combining consulting, software, and hardware were appearing in the market in the late 1990s under the banner of supply chain visibility. Notable early solution providers included Descartes, G-Log, Logility, and Viewlocity. All these visibility solutions came to market in the 1997 to 2000 time period. It seems reasonable to then talk about two phases of supply chain visibility as a term. The first phase starts at least in the 1980s and extends to the late 1990s, and where researchers and practitioners referred to supply chain visibility as a quality being measured, akin to the cost or asset intensiveness of the supply chain. Then in the 1997 to 2000 time frame, coincidental with the rise of standard (but competitive) offerings in the market place which combined software, hardware, and consulting services, researchers and practitioners

Table 1.1   Selected timeline of research on supply chain visibility

Year	Author	Title	Research
1995	Bytheway	Information in the supply chain: measuring supply chain performance.	A brief article which is most interesting in that it lists a number of novel (for the time) uses of information sharing which were just becoming viable due to improved technical capabilities for capture, transmission, and integration of the data.
1997	Closs, Goldsby, and Clinton	Information technology influences on world class logistics capability.	The interaction between material management processes and information exchange processes. This article explains the perceived roadblocks to operationally-effective visibility.
1999	Balakrishnan, Kumara, and Sundaresan	Manufacturing in the digital age: exploiting information technologies for product realization.	Posits that supply chain visibility is largely providing two solutions: Faster and more complete data to support decision making. Access and involvement by more stakeholders in the decision making processes.
2000	Joshi	Information visibility and its effect on supply chain dynamics.	Abstract definition of supply chain visibility as a solution and process, encompassing three steps: A mechanism to locate an object. A mechanism to gather relevant data on the object. A mechanism to interface the relevant data with other IT applications.
2001	Zhao, Dröge, and Stank	The effects of logistics capabilities on firm performance customer-focused versus information-focused capabilities.	Presents results showing that business performance correlates directly with logistics IT investments only when those IT initiatives are purposed to a more fundamental business goal.
2001	McAdam and McCormack	Integrating business processes for global alignment and supply chain management.	The importance of information exchange between independent and autonomous supply chain partners in order to optimize supply chain processes. Also, a focus on the tactical needs of information management, such as ensuring the right information gets to the right person within an organization.
2002	Montgomery, Holcomb, and Manrodt	Visibility: tactical solutions, strategic implications.	A brief account of the kinds of visibility projects being undertaken in the years 2000 to 2002. This provides a decent starting point for normative studies in supply chain visibility around the turn of the millennium.
2003	Mason, Ribera, Farris, and Kirk	Integrating the warehousing and transportation functions of the supply chain.	An early look at the impact at fixed sites (namely warehouses) when transport visibility is made available to the staff and systems. Successfully predicted actual projects undertaken in most global import supply chains in the 2000s.

Table 1.1 Continued

Year	Author	Title	Research
2004	Barlow and Li	Online value network linkages: integration, information sharing and flexibility.	An early work on the potential business impacts from supply chain visibility, particularly for manufacturers.
2005	Småros, Lahtonen, Appelqvist, and Holmström	The impact of increasing demand visibility on production and inventory control efficiency.	Assessment of visibility as a counteracting tool against the Forrester (or "bullwhip") effect and similar phenomena in the supply chain.
2006	Cooper	Textile and apparel supply chain management technology adoption: The Burlington industries case and beyond.	A great review of the (now defunct) US textile and apparel industry and their early adoption of supply chain technologies, including antecedents to modern visibility. Definitely worth reading for professionals close to this industry.
2006	Auramo	IMPLICATIONS OF SUPPLY CHAIN VISIBILITY: BENEFITS IN TRANSACTION EXECUTION AND RESOURCE NETWORK MANAGEMENT	A thesis which works to identify and understand different perspectives of supply chain visibility.
2007	Aberdeen Group	A view from above: global supply chain visibility in a world gone flat.	Reviews the correlations between business performance, supply chain organizational focus, and the presence of visibility solutions.
2007	Barratt and Oke	Antecedents of supply chain visibility in retail supply chains: A resource based theory perspective.	As the title implies, a look at the fundamental building blocks to supply chain visibility for the retail industry. Probably the most important aspect of the research is the finding that only two variables (information quality and relationship commitment) were significantly correlated with strategic-level information exchange.
2007	Fawcett, Osterhaus, Magnan, Brau, and McCarter	Information sharing and supply chain performance: The role of connectivity and willingness.	The criticality of organizational factors, particularly willingness to change, on the outcomes in supply chain visibility initiatives.

Table 1.1   Continued

Year	Author	Title	Research
2008	Hoffman and Hellström	Connectivity in logistics and supply chain management: a framework.	A summary paper on the state of research in supply chain connectivity. This paper is interesting in several respects. First, it introduces a viable model for how organizational factors enable a technologically capable supply chain to move from connectivity to visibility. Second, it identifies the fact that most research focuses on either internal connectivity of the firm or the overall connectivity of the supply chain, but almost no research is done on intra-supply chain clusters or bi-party connectivity.
2008	Johansson and Melin	Supply chain visibility: The value of information.	An attempt to quantify the business performance impacts which accrue to a company when they deploy supply chain visibility.
2009	IBM	THE SMARTER SUPPLY CHAIN OF THE FUTURE	A survey of chief supply chain officers which identified visibility as a top concern but not a top priority for 2009.
2010	Adielsson and Gustavsson	Applying supply chain visibility.	A case study on how supply chain visibility was attempted to be leveraged to improve warehouse and inventory level performance.
2012	Cap Gemini	Supply chain visibility: insight in software solutions.	Reviews the market for SaaS or licensed visibility software along many dimensions. The only side-by-side review of these options available to the public, it appears.
2012	Aberdeen Group	Supply chain visibility excellence: mastering complexity and landed cost.	Reviews the correlations between business performance, supply chain organizational focus, and the presence of visibility solutions.

began to talk about supply chain visibility as an activity to be undertaken; a specific agenda of actions which could improve supply chain performance.

Between the years 2000 and 2013 there has not been a second pivotal shift in the meaning of supply chain visibility. But there also has not been consistency among practitioners or researchers about its definition, which remains somewhat ambiguous in the literature. Despite the ambiguity of definition there has been continued interest in it as a solution to mediate specific supply chain problems. For example, in the IBM Chief Supply Chain Officer study of 2009, supply chain visibility was named as the top challenge to the supply chain organization, ahead of cost control and risk management (IBM, 2009).

HOW IS SUPPLY CHAIN VISIBILITY DEFINED?

Definitions of supply chain visibility are hard to come by in academic sources. As a construct, it is often intermixed with terminology such as traceability and connectivity (Hoffman and Hellström, 2008). Even when a researcher has published a clear definition of visibility, it is often not picked up by subsequent researchers. One definition that has been reused is as follows:

> *Supply chain visibility is the capability of a supply chain player to have access to or to provide the required timely information/knowledge about the entities involved in the supply chain from/to relevant supply chain partners for better decision support (Goh et al., 2009; Adielsson and Gustavsson, 2010).*

Among practitioners the term is also poorly defined, as one of the interviewees noted:

> *If you put twenty people in a room and ask them to define supply chain you get a wide variety of answers. The same thing happens with the term supply chain visibility (Wilkie, Appendix A).*

The ambiguity around the term definition is not helpful. As another practitioner put it:

> *People tend to get latched on to their personal definition of supply chain visibility, and they have trouble accepting other definitions. People tend to be hardwired on this subject (Wilcox, Appendix A).*

As mentioned in the history of the term, early uses of supply chain visibility were informal and denoted a quality of the supply chain under consideration, similar to the supply chain's cost or resilience. Since the late 1990s, the usage has been more purposeful and has indicated a (loosely defined) agenda or solution which, when deployed, improves the performance of the supply chain. For example, there was an early formal model of supply chain visibility as a solution which relied on three layers of business processes (Joshi, 2000):

- A mechanism to locate an object.

- A mechanism to gather relevant data on the object.

- A mechanism to interface the relevant data with other IT applications.

To get closer to a research definition of supply chain visibility, let's enumerate five common axioms which seem to have given it a shared meaning among users of the term since the late 1990s:

1. Visibility means increased awareness of the states of the supply chain activities and related events.

2. Visibility is inward looking: it is not focused on becoming more aware about competitor supply chains, for example.

3. Visibility offers the power to convene facts but not to control actions, it provides awareness but not execution.

4. Visibility is in service of both tactical decisions and strategic decisions.

5. Visibility is achieved through a combination of process and technical means.

HOW DOES SUPPLY CHAIN VISIBILITY WORK?

Beyond definition statements, considerable research has gone into the "how" of supply chain visibility. This research looks for the mechanisms underlying supply chain visibility and why it appears to improve supply chain management. Supply chain visibility is supposed to operate as a decision-support for those individuals or teams managing the supply chain operations. It improves the decision making by simplifying it, accelerating it, reducing the chances of failure, or improving the completeness of the group involved. Reducing complexity, for example, is one commonly cited expectation behind how visibility brings value to the supply chain management team (Aberdeen group, 2012). An early summary of this view states that supply chain visibility is largely doing two things (Balakrishnan, Kumara, and Sundaresan, 1999):

- Faster and more complete data to support decision making.

- Access and involvement by more stakeholders in the decision-making processes.

The mechanics of supply chain visibility tend to rely on a view of supply chains as a series of known sequential steps spread out in geography and time. This view focuses the solution's attention and resources on succedent interdependencies, coordination by planning, and a constrained view of likely alternative outcomes (Baig and Khan, 2001). In other words, most approaches to supply chain visibility *as a solution* take as a founding principle the fact that the supply chain is a series of events or states occurring over time, and that these states and events are almost entirely deterministically linked, such that if a supply chain manager knows enough facts about the current state of events they can predict outcomes into the near future based on deterministic rules. This is the Newtonian view of the universe applied to supply chains: mechanically deterministic without much room for true stochastic variations. It's likely that less deterministic solution approaches will emerge in the future, particularly into supply chain contexts where the probabilistic effects outweigh the deterministic.

To the extent that supply chains really are this deterministic and knowable, supply chain visibility's primary output is to illuminate the mechanics at play and help run the deterministic rules forward so as to predict future supply chain states of interest. Drawing on Baig and Khan (2001), these would generally be three distinct mechanisms:

1. Chronological dependencies between events or states. Once supply chain visibility identifies these, or leverages known dependencies to predict future states, the supply chain managers can respond with better planning.

2.   Mutual dependency of shared resources. Once supply chain visibility identifies these events or states the supply chain managers can respond with better standardization (to optimize the dependency) or with intentional efforts to eliminate the need for shared resources.

3.   Interdependency between supply chain actors. Once supply chain visibility identifies to what extent the behavior of one firm affects other firms in the supply chain the supply chain managers can respond with better formal or informal collaboration or control techniques to ensure beneficial behavior.

The academic literature points to supply chain visibility as being a mix of technology and organizational policies or processes (Auramo, 2006). This parallels the practitioner's world where visibility initiatives are a mix of process re-engineering and technology adoption. Visibility solutions are also applied to both transaction-level decision making and network-design level choices (Auramo, 2006). Although not separated formally, research into supply chain visibility tends to group the target of those solutions into upstream operational activities, and downstream customer responsiveness. These two focuses developed into poles of attentional focus in the larger supply chain management community as well: efficiency vs. effectiveness, pull vs. push, etc. The upstream visibility focus tends to be used by supply chain managers driving towards greater efficiency, hence lower assets or costs for the same output (Småros, Lahtonen, Appelqvist, and Holmström, 2005). The downstream visibility focus is better suited to supply chain management searching for more effective supply chains, hence higher customer satisfaction rates and qualities like agility and resilience (Småros, 2005). One of the best known examples of downstream-focused supply chain visibility was the "Retail Link" system deployed by Wal-Mart with its suppliers starting in 1990. The major purpose of this program was the sharing of daily Point of Sales data with suppliers and the transfer of responsibility for stock-level management to that supplier, sometimes as formal VMI and sometimes under other terms of ownership (Småros, 2005). The results of this program are almost legend among retailers in North America. Wal-Mart was able to reduce operating costs, asset levels, and stock-out situations simultaneously. The result was a landslide market share win, leaving Wal-Mart the largest retailer in the world. But the investment had been at a similar level: supporting the exchange of all this data was a private satellite network Wal-Mart had completed in 1988, the largest private satellite network in the world at the time.

Upstream Visibility:
- Finished goods inventory
- Capacity
- On-order and In-transit
- Credit exposure
- Raw material position

Downstream Visibility:
- Feedback on quality
- Plan vs. actual sales for seasonal or new products
- Channel inventory
- Point of Sale Demand

Figure 1.2   Upstream vs. downstream visibility focus

Implicitly, supply chain visibility requires quality information in order to be effective. In fact, research suggests that at least in those industries where the issue is well surveyed, data quality and organizational willingness seem to be the only two factors significantly correlated with positive business outcomes from visibility projects (Barratt and Oke, 2007). In this context, quality of information can be generalized to mean the extent to which the information meets the needs of the organization (Zhou and Benton Jr., 2007). Challenging to quantify, the quality of data is often given as a reason why supply chain visibility projects are not started or are halted before completion.

Organizational Factors in Supply Chain Visibility

Supply chain visibility is achieved as a combination of process and technology, and in both domains the organization factors surrounding a visibility project will be pivotal. These can include the typical project topics of executive sponsorship, reservation of resources, cross-functional team leadership, and risk adversity. But the academic research on supply chain visibility suggests two organizational factors are highly correlated with successful visibility initiatives (Barratt and Oke, 2007). These are *information quality* and *organizational commitment*.

INFORMATION QUALITY

Information quality (or the more common term "data quality") can be generally defined as the extent to which the information meets the needs of the organization (Zhou and Benton Jr., 2007). More directly, it can be quantified along dimensions such as:

- accuracy;

- trust;

- timeliness;

- usability.

If it seems surprising that data quality is considered an organizational factor as opposed to a technology factor, it may be useful to review research regarding quality in general. Quality is an emergent property, asymptotically derived from the myriad processes executed in the organization. Many of those processes are indeed supported by technology, but the technology is operated to the purposes of the organization, and within its bounds of values, constraints, and goals. In short, organizations with little or weak technology can produce superb quality and organizations with cutting edge technology can produce poor quality data.

To give a supply chain example of this difference in the origins of quality, consider the Dabbawala of Mumbai. They are a group of lunch deliverymen who operate in the metro area, offering a service where they pick up a boxed lunch from a worker's home (usually made by their stay-at-home relatives) and bring it to their place of work, then return back after lunch to collect the box and bring it to their home again. This is incredibly labor intensive and a logistical nightmare. Over a hundred thousand pickup and delivery points per day, each with only one consignment (i.e. very little chance of economy of scales through batching), fast transit time requirements, and material handling units which all look identical but must be managed as unique.

Despite being mostly illiterate and having no technology in their supply chain process, the Dabbawala managed to achieve Six Sigma certification (Moore, 2011). To be more precise, this indicates the illiterate and technologically unsophisticated deliverymen of Mumbai are taking orders, picking up packaged food boxes, sorting them at multiple hubs, executing final delivery, and then doing the entire reverse logistics process with only one in six million deliveries being late or misdirected. At a throughput of around 130,000 lunches per day they are averaging six to seven mistakes per year. In contrast, a 2005 supply chain study in the USA retail industry found that the corresponding quality rate for supplier order fulfillment was 22 percent (Supply Chain Visions, 2005).

It's hard to overemphasize the qualitative difference between these two examples. For one thing, in the Dabbawala situation it took outside observers to calculate the rate of fulfillment failure, because the people managing this supply chain lacked the skills to even measure themselves. In the USA retailer situation all parties had the requisite IT systems to measure themselves and were fully aware of their poor performance. Rather than viewing the incredible achieved quality of the Dabbawala as a fluke of luck, some researchers have given credible analysis which point to organizational factors. According to Stefan Thomke, co-author of the Harvard case study on the Dabbawala system:

> Initially (we) assumed that the secret was in the operating system, in the way the Dabbawalas managed material and information flows. But it turns out, much of their success can be attributed to their human resource system—the way they hire, develop, manage, and reward people. It's an organization built around people, not around technology. It is very different from the organizations that our students study every day. It challenges their assumptions about the drivers of performance. The Dabbawala system works because of its people not because of technology or sophisticated management (Tan, 2011).

Some specific aspects which seem to be driving quality in this scenario are:

1. Shared reward/losses.

2. Social pressure to achieve high quality.

3. Lifelong consequences for failure (the Dabbawala all come from a small set of villages, are mostly related, and enter the trade for life).

4. Social reward and praise for achieved quality.

5. Prioritization of quality over profit (they maintain significant redundancy in order to be agile and resilient).

What does all this discussion about quality mean for supply chain visibility? The main things to remember as a practitioner are two simple points: First, data quality is significantly correlated with overall supply chain visibility success. Second, data quality is primarily an organizational as opposed to technical topic. One way a reader can integrate the evaluation of data quality in to a visibility project is simply to use the supply chain visibility scorecard suggested in this book. In the scorecard, the sensitivity category helps identify if the data is accurate and timely, and the accessibility category assesses if it is usable. Generally speaking, if the team working on the visibility project ranks an option high in these scorecard dimensions, data quality is probably not the top concern. If a certain situation requires deeper quality evaluation, the scorecard can be amended to allow for this.

ORGANIZATIONAL COMMITMENT

Through the history of research into supply chain visibility there has been a significant part of the agenda focused on organizational willingness to make the necessary changes for success (Closs, Goldsby, and Clinton, 1997). Later work targeted at this particular topic showed that significant failures can occur in visibility projects when the organizational willingness is lacking (Fawcett et al., 2007). Probably most telling is the fact that firms which directed their resources and attention to customer-focused initiatives had high correlation with business performance but that firms which directed resources and attention to information technology initiatives did not (Zhao, Dröge, and Stank, 2001). What this line of research indicated was that the investment in IT had to be within a context of a larger goal which had organizational backing. In short, IT investment is a means to achieve other goals rather than a goal itself for the most effective organizations (Zhao, Dröge, and Stank, 2001).

Industry practitioners gave feedback on the importance of organizational factors, such as this comment:

> It's first a strategy question, then a business process question, and third a technology question. In point of fact, you must define "what is the strategy for the supply chain and overall organization, right down to the relation (to the relation) to the customer." You need sponsorship right from the top, right from the CEO. That's priority number one. Then the onus of the process is on supply chain leadership, as they understand the processes and implications. And secondarily the CIO, who understands the legacy systems and also how the infrastructure needs to be adapted (Wilkie, Appendix A).

For those who have been lucky enough to avoid overly political work environments a logical question might be "why would an organization *not* be willing to make the requisite changes accompanying a new visibility initiative"? In reality, supply chain visibility tends to lead to deep changes in the organizations which deploy it seriously. As noted in studies on actual deployments among manufacturers, visibility technology can be a *transformer* of businesses more than an *enabler* (Balakrishnan, Kumara, and Sundaresan, 1999). Naturally any deep transformation of an organization leaves uncertainty for the participants, and both the academic literature and practitioner view is that change in the workplace scares the majority of people. Not surprisingly, change management was identified in some research on supply chain visibility as a critical factor to achieving successful outcomes (Cap Gemini, 2012).

The difference between capability and willingness is best shown in a framework derived from work by Hoffman and Hellström in 2008 which shows the relationships between inputs leading to supply chain visibility. They draw a distinction which other research supports as meaningful: connection is not the same as visibility (Fawcett et al., 2007). Connectivity could be defined as the capacity to share information, whereas visibility is a higher order action which assumes capacity to share but also requires that the shared information result in new and different decision outcomes. This distinction appeared in practitioner interviews, such as in this statement:

> *A lot of people consider EDI their visibility tool. Five years ago this was a good starting point, but it's not the solution that is needed today. For the customers that were the most successful they have broken down the technical barriers and look past the "how do I get the data" such as EDI messages and instead focus on the end result and what business processes are being driven, and then backing in to how you will get the data needed (Fenwick, Appendix A).*

In their research and resulting framework, the presence of organizational willingness is a requisite enabler to move from being connected to achieving supply chain visibility (Hoffman and Hellström, 2008).

COMPETITIVE ADVANTAGE CONFERRED BY VISIBILITY

One research question of interest is if visibility itself leads to competitive advantages for the company who deploys it. Enough time has passed for fairly long-term studies on the correlations between visibility in the supply chain and individual or supply chain level competitive advantage. Some of this research focused on the more general processes of collaboration and data sharing between supply chain partners: something one would identify as visibility but which was not named as such in the original studies. But other research has been more specific and looked at self-identified "visibility" initiatives and their correlated outcomes.

There is a known distinction in IT-driven projects that some kinds of technology will tend to drive competitive advantage of an industry, region, or supply chain without necessarily improving the individual competitive position of a given firm (Carr, 2003). Carr referred to technologies which can be controlled and leveraged by only one firm, or those it gives permission to, as "proprietary technologies," perhaps an overly loaded term in today's context. But his points on broadly available "infrastructure" technologies have aged better. There certainly are some technologies which advance all or most competitors in parallel, making the market radically different but not necessarily giving any one player an advantage. Is supply chain visibility like this?

It seems to depend on the industry. In industries such as retail the presence and effectiveness of supply chain visibility has been an enormous determinant of the ability to get the right product to the right store at the right time and price it in an effective way: as was proven by the famous "Retail Link" visibility system of Wal-Mart starting in 1990 (Småros, 2005). This system depended on massive investment in technology and process changes but laid the foundation for the growth of Wal-Mart into the largest retailer in the world. Other industries, such as logistics services, show visibility initiatives giving some players an early-adopter lead but that those advantages were short lived. Probably the most known case of a logistics service provider earning a competitive advantage through supply chain visibility is FedEx's early adoption of barcode scanning combined with online track and trace of parcel deliveries. But this also serves as an example of how supply chain visibility competitive advantages in this industry vertical were quickly eroded through broad adoption of similar capabilities.

In terms of how much benefit can be derived from supply chain visibility, there are a number of published figures, but these all show correlation as opposed to a causal link between visibility and business outcomes. In the 2009 Chief Supply Chain Officer study by IBM, they singled out 17 out of nearly 40 executives who lead supply chains listed in the "AMR Research Supply Chain Top 25 for 2008" (IBM, 2009). Contrasting the performance of the top supply chains to the others, IBM reported that every one of the top performing supply chains was engaged in significant visibility projects and that 60 percent of them had completed or were rolling out every major type of visibility solution they discussed in the interview questionnaire (IBM, 2009). Along similar lines, an Aberdeen Group study from 2007 evaluated correlations between visibility initiatives and overall supply chain performance (Aberdeen Group, 2007). They defined best-in-class supply chains based on their changes and absolute performance in four metrics: perfect order delivery to customers, perfect order receipt from suppliers, reduction of supply chain management costs, and reduction in supply chain lead time variability (Aberdeen Group, 2007). They reported that best-in-class supply chains (those in the top 20 percent of the studied cohort) were 55 percent more likely to leverage supply chain visibility solutions. The savings from supply chain visibility for those firms studied was over $500,000 USD for more than half the respondents, compared to median annual revenues around $500 million USD (Aberdeen Group, 2007).

In another study by the Aberdeen group five years later they explained the differences between best in class and laggard supply chains as such:

> Compared to laggards, best in class companies have twenty-three percent higher complete and on-time delivery rates and eleven percent better landed costs. They are also 2.5 times more likely to have a visibility in to customs events and 1.7 times more likely to have visibility to supply disruptions (Aberdeen Group, 2012).

The same study lists other important correlations between supply chain operations, business performance, and supply chain visibility. The results cannot prove causation (they lack a control group, for example) but they certainly indicate that stronger supply chains are more likely to leverage supply chain visibility. One notable point was that the correlation between best-in-class business performance and supply chain visibility initiatives was strongest for customer-focuses visibility (i.e. downstream) rather than supplier-focused (i.e. upstream) (Aberdeen Group, 2012).

In an excellent study which tracked a series of companies before and after they instituted visibility solutions (with varying degrees of success), significant financial gains were seen for all successful implementations (Johansson and Melin, 2008). In this study the financial impacts were quantified as changes to the return on assets, and results varied from two to five percentage point increases (Johansson and Melin, 2008). For those not familiar with the return on assets methodology, this is a broad way to assess an organization's financial impact from visibility. In effect it is the profit (i.e. return on costs) divided by the assets held to generate that profit. In finance literature this is also sometimes called the "economic value add" when reported as an absolute figure instead of a percentage. As a metric for supply chain visibility financial impact it covers the ability to increase revenue, reduce costs, and reduce inventory levels. Results from the study show increases of two to five percentage points, but many of these companies began with single-digit return on assets to begin with (Johansson and Melin, 2008). So, for example, a company that begins with 8 percent return on assets and increased by four percentage points has had a subjective improvement of 50 percent (Johansson and Melin, 2008).

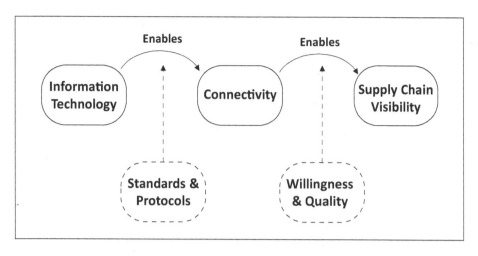

Figure 1.3   Organization factors leading from technology to visibility

2

A Novel Framework: Definition, Prerequisites, and Scorecarding

The current state of supply chain visibility research and the theory it has generated has at least three significant deficits that are acute pressure points on practitioners trying to build visibility solutions. The first weakness is in the ambiguity and variety of definitions of supply chain visibility. A weak definition may not seem like a significant impediment, but in projects where organizational change management is required it's vital that the organization share a common meaning behind the terms they are using. Beyond just alignment on a shared meaning, supply chain visibility needs to be defined more comprehensively (i.e. at greater levels of abstraction), while also focusing attention on the practical aspects of visibility, such as how it can be measured and improved.

Second, there is a need for clear theoretical guidance of what are the prerequisites for successful supply chain visibility. This is particularly important for practitioners because they are staking enterprise resources, their organizational power, and their own time and career into visibility projects. They need to know if the project is unviable from the start because a key prerequisite is missing.

Third, it is not yet clear how supply chain visibility should be measured, both in terms of itself and its impacts on the overall business. Whereas several lines of research seem to verify high correlation between overall business performance and the presence of supply chain visibility, they haven't directly addressed the question of metrics of success. What dimensions are appropriate for quantifying supply chain visibility or its impacts? Most importantly, what dimensions would allow practitioners to compare and contrast different visibility solutions, options, or variations in a fair way?

Taken together these three areas of weakness in the current theoretical understanding of supply chain visibility have significant impacts on industry practitioners. They increase the risk of visibility projects and slow down the ability to identify and share best practices. In the remainder of this chapter a novel approach to these three topics is presented. First is a definitional framework for supply chain visibility, one that is abstract but also specific regarding the process steps needed. Following this is a proposal for the specific factors which should be evaluated as prerequisites for successful supply chain visibility. Lastly, there is a proposed supply chain visibility scorecard which includes metrics and methodology for evaluating supply chain visibility. The proposed supply chain visibility scorecard should enable the comparison of different visibility solutions. Together these three proposals form a new theoretical framework for effective visibility: how it's defined, what it requires, and how its success is measured.

A New Definition of Supply Chain Visibility

It's proposed that supply chain visibility can be defined as:

> *A process of four meta-steps: capture data, integrate data, create intelligence, and interrupt decisions. Either the data being collected or the decisions being interrupted should be supply-chain oriented, and should span outside of a single organization's boundaries.*

This definition is abstract enough to go across industries, but still focuses attention on the meta-steps in the process which can be usefully critiqued and compared across visibility solutions. The first sentence of the definition may appear too broad if taken in isolation. With the first sentence alone one

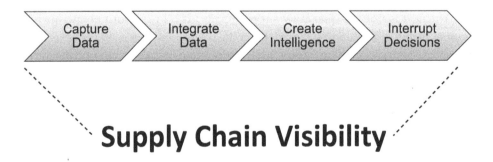

Figure 2.1   The meta-steps of supply chain visibility

could conflate supply chain visibility with business intelligence, for example. The second sentence is needed to distinguish supply chain visibility from any other enterprise visibility. It should be clear that the "supply chain" part of the term indicates in what domain the whole process is taking place, and that means either the data collected is coming from supply chain activities or the decisions being interrupted are oriented at supply chain activities. Being based on supply chain means the source data almost always deals with the flow of material, information, or capital across independent trading partners who add value to a final purchase and who must somehow share the ultimate sale's revenue. Although the model of data collection, integration, intelligence creation, and decision interruption could apply to medical surgery, we would never refer to that as supply chain visibility because it does not involve a *supply chain*.

Also, supply chain visibility probably should not cover detailed warehouse operations, such as a system-directed put-away of materials, even though it technically meets the definition provided in the first sentence and is also supply chain related. This adds one more qualifier to the definition: supply chain visibility should be targeted at cross-organizational processes. This qualifier feels right to many practitioners because it explains why visibility to an upstream supplier's warehouse inventory levels is considered an example of supply chain visibility, whereas the same data about a company's own warehouse inventory level is considered just normal ERP or accounting. So, to recap, supply chain visibility is *a process of collecting supply chain data, integrating it, extracting intelligence from it, and using that intelligence to interrupt decisions in a cross-organizational supply chain oriented context.*

For those who prefer bullet points, the supply chain visibility definition would look like this:

- A four-step process of:

  - data collection;
  - data integration;
  - intelligence extraction;
  - decision interruption.

- Supply chain oriented, at least in the first or last step.

- Cross-organization span of process.

If this seems too abstract, it's possible to understand the definition of supply chain visibility by way of analogy. Here we can think of a commercial airplane and the pilot as an example of a supply chain and its management. Flying at 1,200 kilometers per hour and carrying hundreds of passengers, the modern wide-body aircraft is a feat of engineering. All across the plane are sensors to capture wind speed and direction, altitude, fuel level, and the internal and external air pressure. Modern planes are built with non-serial duplicated sensors, so for every measurement there is at least one other sensor making the same measurement and compiling its data in isolation. These data streams are sent in to the avionics computers onboard, which integrate the data and store it in formats which are needed for later access. Some of the data that the avionics computers are working with are direct measurements of a physical state, like GPS coordinates or altitude. But others are more abstract, such as the estimated flight path and estimated fuel efficiency. By combining the data in specific ways the avionics computers create intelligence, such as when they realize the plane is too far from its destination to arrive with current fuel levels and expected fuel efficiency. Important intelligence like this can then help the pilot in making correct decisions.

Procedurally, what happens in the plane analogy is what we see in supply chain visibility. In many supply chains, the management team act like pilots overseeing a large and expensive machine. The supply chain operation generates enormous, often redundant, data streams. For example, when a delivery occurs we can presume that both the transporter and the recipient have a transactional record of the exchange. As the data streams are collected, exchanged, and processed the data must be reconciled and interconnected. By analysis, the massively interconnected data can then produce intelligence. As in the plane example, the intelligence often comes from comparing expected values to actual values. Finally the supply chain managers need the intelligence about what is happening to interrupt them when it's time to make decisions. This could be as a chart on a report which is printed just before a supplier meeting, on a dashboard which is visible to a transport manager every morning, or as an SMS sent to the COO's mobile phone when all operations close due to a typhoon. A softer wording would be to say that the intelligence "supports" the decision maker. But by using the more aggressive tone of "interruption" we focus our attention on the fact that a decision *must* be interrupted in a way that leads to a new and better decision or else the visibility process was useless. Again, by way of analogy, if the airplane is sounding alarms for low fuel or low altitude and the pilots behave exactly as they would have without this signal, what value was the signal (and therefore the entire process leading to it)? This metaphor also shows the relationship between technology and visibility, which is a topic of considerable interest to practitioners. In practitioner interviews and also in the academic research the consensus is that visibility is dependent on technology but not a technology topic itself. As one interviewee stated:

> ... *it's inherently a process where technology is important but not all encompassing. You must first understand your own business goals and processes, and then use technology tools to facilitate those processes (Karel, Appendix A).*

Leaving behind the aircraft example, here are true supply chain circumstances where the definition of visibility can be seen in operation.

- A delivery driver gets a proof of delivery signature (Data Capture) from the customer. At the end of the day, a clerk scans the paper receipt into a document server (Data Capture again). The Document Server saves the proof of delivery signature with the document ID number created to be the same as the shipment number (Interconnect Data). At the end of the month the transporter's accounting team runs a report for all shipments with a proof of delivery document (Create Intelligence). This shipment list is then used to create a combined invoice, while the shipments without a PDF are invoiced separately because they will be paid slower because the shipper audits them differently (Interrupt Decisions).

- A buyer revises a PO in her ERP system (data capture). The PO is interfaced to a web portal application managed by a third party agent (Interconnect Data). The agent's system identifies if the PO is a new order or a revised order (create intelligence). Since it is a revised order, the system checks to see if the changes relate to the supplier, the agent, or the transporter (create intelligence). Since the changes relate to the expected ship dates, the system notifies both the transporter and the supplier that a PO has been updated (interrupt decisions). The notification to the supplier is an email, with a link to approve or reject the changes. When the supplier replies, their response is used to update the PO (capture data), to send updates to the buyer's ERP system (interconnect data), and if the supplier declines the change the system notifies the buyer by email and SMS so they do not expect the merchandise on the proposed dates (interrupt decisions).

- Four buyers, in different divisions of a large company, enter high-value POs for the same supplier in their ERP systems (data capture). The orders are in separate ERP systems, but their data is interfaced to a visibility application managed centrally (interconnect data). A separate department manages counterparty credit risk. Each month they set a maximum liability limit for all trading partners, upstream and downstream (capture data). This information is interfaced to the visibility application (interconnect data). The application runs ongoing checks to ensure total on-order value meets the risk-management's limits for the related party (create intelligence). When this check shows that the four orders placed by the buyers would lead to an unacceptable risk, the system looks up the buyers who wrote the POs (interconnect data) and the risk manager who submitted the company-specific limit (interconnect data), and the visibility system sends them all a group email containing the necessary report or summary of PO and credit-limit activities (interrupt decisions).

- An oil rig engineer is working in a multi-rig field, checking on the machinery. To start her inspection the engineer scans a barcode indicating which rig she is working on (data capture). She notes a repair that should be made by entering a work order on a mobile device (data capture). While the engineer drives back towards the nearest town the device syncs up with a remote server (interconnect data). The visibility application integrates the data, including the connection between the repair order and the rig ID (interconnect data). The visibility application also looks up the GPS coordinates for the rig (interconnect data) and finds the nearest authorized maintenance company (interconnect data). This maintenance company is now issued a repair order (create intelligence). Finally, the repair technician goes to execute the repair but is blocked from marking the transaction as complete unless her GPS-enabled mobile device is within a specific radius of the target rig (interrupt decisions). This prevents the repairs from being done on the wrong rig in the field, wasting parts, time, and allowing risk of rig failure to increase.

CONTRASTING THE PROPOSED DEFINITION TO PREVIOUS DEFINITIONS

Most previous supply chain visibility definitions are similar to the one being proposed here. The notable differences are as follows. First, unlike the majority of the academic literature on visibility, this definition does not assume that supply chain visibility must be inward facing. In other words, one could have supply chain visibility on a competitor's supply chain. This is not an abstract idea, it is already happening in practice. As an example, software as a service provider Panjiva sells supply chain visibility tools which are focused on competitor's supply chains. Second, the proposed definition provides a concrete four-step process which can be used to critique or contrast supply chain visibility solutions. Each of those steps has a specific input and output, and therefore it is relatively easy to devise metrics for their effectiveness and efficiency. Third, the definition uses the more aggressive terminology of "interruption" to focus attention on the fact that different and better decisions should emerge from the visibility process. It is not simply about "knowing" the state of the supply chain but about changing decisions with that knowledge. In terms of similarities, this new definition extends previous work which saw visibility as a decision support (Goh et al., 2009; Adielsson and Gustavsson, 2010) and also extends the three-step process outlined by Joshi (2000). Most importantly, it aligns with earlier work which specifically saw visibility as a combination of processes which rely on technological and organizational resources (Fawcett et al., 2007). In academic circles the need for both organizational and technological resources for successful supply chain visibility is broadly confirmed. But practitioners tend to overlook the organizational aspects and treat visibility as mostly about technology. In other words, there is a tendency to confuse the requisite tools (usually technology) with the underlying process. In the examples given above (and in all the examples discussed in this book) the same supply chain visibility process can be done without advanced technology. For example, using GPS locations to lock-down the risk of a repair on the wrong oil rig could be done just as well by painting a long string of random letters on the oil rig somewhere. When the repairman starts to do his work, he must call back to the office and read the random letters for a correct match with the expected match from company records. Even lower-tech strategies could be used: give the repairman only one key which unlocks the cabinet for the target rig, so that if he arrives on the wrong rig they will not be able to proceed with their task. The fact that supply chain visibility is defined as a process combining technological and organization resources is a good thing, because supply chain management has a wealth of tools for dealing with these kinds of processes. As a field, supply chain management is process oriented much more than technology oriented.

PREREQUISITES FOR SUPPLY CHAIN VISIBILITY SUCCESS

The second component of the proposed framework is a clear understanding of prerequisites needed for successful supply chain visibility initiatives in practical settings. The academic literature on this subject is thin, but some research has been made and it tends to suggest the following aspects have a high correlation with successful business impacts:

1.   Connectivity capabilities.

2.   Organizational willingness.

3.   Organizational focus (effectiveness vs. efficiency).

4.   Technological capability.

5.   Organizational relationship between supply chain partners (conflictive vs. cooperative).

The proposal here is that *connectivity capabilities* and *technological capabilities* are really the same dimension, simply with different levels of granularity. Nothing in the published literature suggests that connectivity capability must be considered independent of technology, so we can reasonably reduce the list accordingly. Also, it seems that the organizational relationship between supply chain partners is an outcome of organizational willingness and focus. This dimension is important for understanding why a *specific instance* of supply chain visibility has succeeded or failed, but is likely not a prerequisite for *all* supply chain visibility. In other words, viable supply chain visibility approaches exist for *conflicting* as well as *cooperating* supply chain relationships. Therefore the dimension of organizational relationships can't be a prerequisite to visibility in general, only to a specific visibility strategy or design. Likewise for the dimension of organizational focus. Research has shown that supply chain organizations benefit from visibility whether their focus is on effectiveness or efficiency, but that certain approaches to visibility work better in each case. Based on this reading of the available research and feedback from practitioners, it's proposed that three factors are truly prerequisite for successful supply chain visibility regardless of how that visibility is implemented:

1.   Technological capability.

2.   Organizational willingness.

3.   Data quality.

These factors influence each other but are sufficiently orthogonal to merit separate attention. Unlike the framework outlined by Hoffman and Hellström

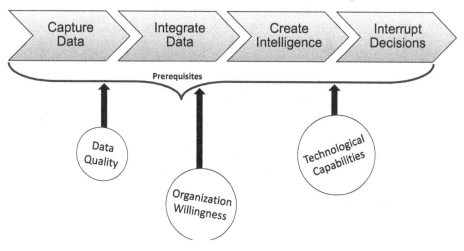

Figure 2.2   The prerequisites to supply chain visibility

in 2008, the model proposed here does not have a linear quality. In other words, it's not true that technology enables data quality which enables in turn the organizational willingness. No other permutation in the sequence of dependency is being proposed either. What the new framework suggests is that there are correlations and influences between the three prerequisites to successful supply chain visibility, but that ultimately they must all be at a satisfactory level at the same time before the visibility process has a chance of being successful.

EVALUATING SUPPLY CHAIN VISIBILITY

Arming oneself with a working definition and an understanding of the prerequisites of success supply chain visibility is important, but there are many ways to implement supply chain visibility, some radically different to each other. How can those options be compared and contrasted effectively? More dauntingly, how can cross-organization comparisons be made, perhaps even cross-industry, in regards to supply chain visibility? In professions such as consulting this is a hot topic, because the process of identifying and deploying best practices relies on the ability to isolate components of successful supply chain operations. The supply chain domain needs metrics that can be used for objective assessment of supply chain visibility. This is, in short, the third major question the new supply chain visibility framework is seeking to answer.

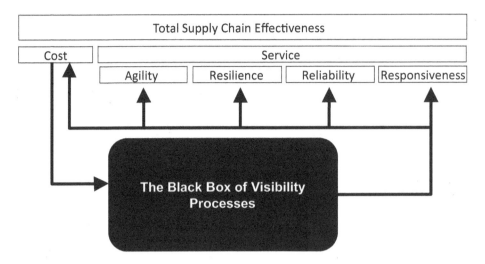

Figure 2.3   Predominant approach to evaluating supply chain visibility
              performance

One logical approach would be to use existing models of overall business
performance to assess the impact of supply chain visibility on the company. This
approach has been used in previous studies (Aberdeen Group, 2007; Johansson
and Melin, 2008; IBM, 2009; Aberdeen Group, 2012). Evaluating supply chain
performance by looking at business performance metrics is widely considered
a valid approach.

The best known benchmarking exercises today take this as their
methodology, including the Supply Chain Council's SCOR-based benchmarking
and the Gartner (formerly AMR) Supply Chain Top 25. Newcomers to this
niche of analysts have critiqued the *formulas* used by the Supply Chain Council
or Gartner (most notably the organization Supply Chain Insights headed by
former AMR vice president on supply chain research Lora Cecere), but the
critiques and suggested revisions still assume that it is valid to measure a
supply chain by the overall business performance. The question then is simple:
is supply chain visibility impactful enough on supply chain operations to
justify the claim that changes in overall business performance can be attributed
to visibility initiatives? In short, if assets decline or revenues increase in the
same period as supply chain visibility initiatives, should we attribute those
improvements to the visibility solution? There are reasons to be skeptical.

The kind of total business performance metrics which are publicly available
and standardized are, by their nature, broad strokes to describe a company. As

an example, public companies may report their inventory stock levels but only in aggregate and only as a value as opposed to units. It may or may not be justified to trace changes of that inventory position to supply chain manager actions, but it's an even weaker link to connect it to a visibility initiative. There seem to be four distinct reasons why this approach can lead to superfluous conclusions:

1. It frames the data in a way that is blind to other initiatives happening in parallel at the company.

2. There is no way to account for the time-lag between the visibility initiative and the results.

3. It takes correlation for causality and lacks a control group to measure against.

4. Even if accurate, it is not instructive about why or how the visibility solution succeeded.

First on the issue of framing: this is perhaps the most pernicious weakness of the approach. In previous research such as Johansson and Melin's study in 2008 the data made available for analysis shows business performance and supply chain visibility maturity. By framing the evaluation in this way it leaves only two possible outcomes: correlation or non-correlation. What is missing but particularly vital is the information about what the rest of the organization or market was doing during the window of analysis, or just prior to it. For example, were logistics sites opening in new markets and adding inventory in preparation for a geographic launch? Was the marketing department trying new pricing or product configurations? Were the sales teams experimenting with different account management structures? These other organizational factors play a significant role in the overall performance of business, and directly impact financial metrics like return on assets, Altman's Z, or inventory turnover. The framing issue, at its roots, comes from either ignorance of the other activities in the company or from an unacknowledged preference to see impact in business performance be dependent on supply chain management.

The second weakness of measuring supply chain visibility in terms of total business performance is the accounting of time-lag between visibility initiatives and business outcomes. The supply chain operation is a set of activities spread in time. Although some steps happen concurrently and the linearity of the supply chain is not as high as the name implies, it is still mostly filled with sequentially dependent activities. Well known supply chain phenomenon such as the Forrester (or "bullwhip") effect occur in part because of time-delays between decisions and decision outcomes. It therefore is quite challenging to accurately connect a financial metric's value at one point in time to visibility solutions which acted at several different points in time along a sequence of activities.

Third, correlation is not causality. This relates to the entire approach of evaluating visibility by business performance, in that it implies that a causal link exists between supply chain and business outcomes. But that is a presumption (albeit one that is widely shared). What could be occurring is that a high *correlation* exists, but that the *causal* link is elsewhere in the business or market. For example, perhaps businesses that have excellent supply chains and excellent business results do so because of their human resource policies which tend to place great people in maximally effective roles. The requisite analysis to discriminate on causal links would include a larger frame of inputs (as discussed in point one above), but also the use of control groups to compare against. In other words, analysts would need a way to assess supply chain initiatives in contrast to non-initiatives within the same context.

Finally, even if the entire exercise of evaluating supply chain visibility by total business performance were validated in terms of framing, causal linkage, and time-delay effects, it still doesn't provide guidance on how or why the visibility initiative was successful. In other words, if this approach is effective it is only effective by treating supply chain visibility as a black-box. That diminishes the utility of the approach because the unit of analysis is so large it cannot guide fine-grain comparisons, critique, or tuning. For example, imagine that two supply chains engage in different visibility initiatives, but have the same impact on their business results. Without more detailed metrics on supply chain visibility it would be impossible to tell what parts of the two different initiatives were contributing most to their success and whether a cross-breed of the two visibility solutions could be made to benefit from the best of both solutions.

The proposed way to address the need for supply chain visibility metrics is to introduce them as sub-metrics to the overall supply chain. This follows the approach adopted in supply chain metrics paradigm such as the SCOR model from the Supply Chain Council. In SCOR metrics, there are level one metrics such as "Perfect Order Fulfilment" which are decomposable in to sub-metrics such as "Percent of Orders Delivered in Full" and "Delivery Performance to Customer Commit Date." The level two metrics can then be decomposed as well in to level three metrics. For example, "Percent of Orders Delivered in Full" is decomposed in to "Delivery Item Accuracy" and "Delivery Quantity

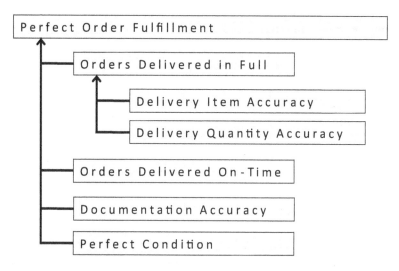

Figure 2.4   SCOR-style supply chain performance metrics

Accuracy." The diagram below shows the structural decomposition for "Perfect Order Fulfillment" and is derived from the SCOR Model Reference 2010 guide (Supply Chain Council, 2010).

The proposal here is to treat supply chain visibility as a vector of influence on the supply chain operation, which in turn is a vector of influence on the business outcomes. This approach is shown graphically below.

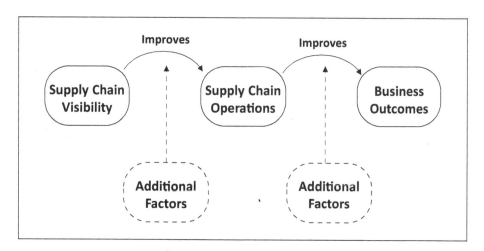

Figure 2.5   Visibility, supply chain, and overall business performance relationships

What this implies is that four specific components can be measured separately:

1.   One can measure the extent to which supply chain operations impact the business outcomes. This is the line of enquiry pursued by Gartner in their annual top 25 supply chain report and also by Supply Chain Insights in their Supply Chain Index. To some extent it is also used in the Supply Chain Council's Benchmarking process.

2.   One can measure the supply chain operation directly. This is the purpose of tools such as the Supply Chain Council's SCOR Metric methodology.

3.   One can measure the extent to which supply chain visibility improves supply chain operations. Not much research has been done in this area, but Johansson and Melin's study in 2008 is an example. It's probably best to use the SCOR Metrics methodology, looking for impacts to level three metrics and add in statistical control groups to isolate causality.

4.   One can measure the supply chain visibility effectiveness directly. This is, at present, an area with no published research. It is this area that is discussed in the proposed "supply chain visibility scorecard" later.

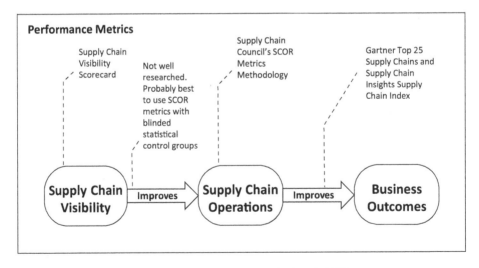

Figure 2.6   **Measuring points for supply chain visibility**

The following metrics and methodology are referred to as the "supply chain visibility scorecard," and they represent a novel approach to measuring the performance of supply chain visibility directly without conflating the metrics with the impact visibility is having on the overall supply chain operation. The scorecard is decomposed in to four primary metrics which directly reflect on the performance of the four steps within supply chain visibility. These metrics are therefore diagnostic tools for assessing the health of the visibility sub-processes. The four metric categories under the visibility fit scorecard are discussed in detail here, and then the scorecard evaluation process is presented.

The first metric of supply chain visibility performance is "sensitivity." This metric covers the first step in the visibility process, i.e. the capture of data. A highly sensitive visibility process is one which very successfully captures supply chain data, and conversely an insensitive visibility process will not capture all the necessary data. The metric of sensitivity decomposes into these kinds of sub-metrics:

- Accuracy and bias.

- Completeness.

- Timeliness.

- Redundancy.

- Depth of detail.

The second metric of supply chain visibility is "accessibility." This metric quantifies how integrated the visibility solution makes its data model. High accessibility implies that a business user may start from any point and find the data they need. It also implies that users can navigate from one object to another object in multiple paths (if they are not a hindrance to usability) and that such navigation is low-cost and fast. Accessibility can be well quantified. Look at the diagram of two data models below and then consider these example metrics of accessibility:

- Do all data objects connect?

- What is the min, average, median, and max node count between any two objects?

- What is the average effort to move through an intermediary node?

- What is the average time to move through an intermediary node?

The design on the right has more data elements, which would make it stronger in the *sensitivity* category. But it is measurably less *accessible*: it has longer average connections between objects and making those connections is slower and more expensive. Accessibility directly measures the effectiveness of the second step in a supply chain visibility process: the integration of captured data. To the extent that this step is well executed, the accessibility of the supply chain visibility solution should be high.

The third performance metric of supply chain visibility is "intelligence." The category "intelligence" refers to the effectiveness of the routines used to process data and render it into relevant information. It measures the third step in the visibility process, the creation of intelligence. In many ways, the intelligence behind a visibility solution is the hardest to measure. In general the intelligence of the visibility solution is quantifiable by these sub-metrics:

- Ability to recognize an event or state as needing or not needing intervention.

- Ease of updating from users to improve the recognition of important business events.

- The ability to learn or develop independently or through implied performance feedback.

The fourth performance metric of the supply chain visibility scorecard is "Decision-Relevance." This category is a measure of how well the visibility solution integrates into business decisions. The decision may be frequent and transactional in nature (like selecting from a list of approved vendors or ship-dates) or may be strategic and infrequent, such as when planning a logistics network after a merger or acquisition. The decision relevance metric directly quantifies the effectiveness of the fourth step of supply chain visibility: the interruption of decisions. The decision relevance can be quantified using these kinds of sub-metrics:

- Is the visibility process or solution required for the decision maker?

- Which party (visibility solution or human decision maker) starts the process of making a decision?

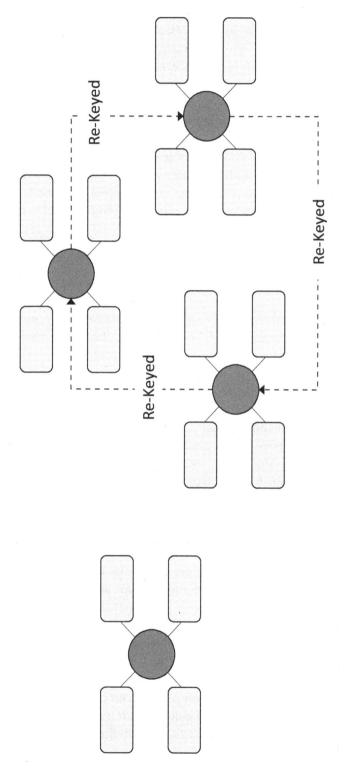

Figure 2.7 Example integration models

- Does the visibility solution offer one or more suggested actions?

- Can the visibility solution execute any actions selected by the decision maker?

- Can the visibility solution fully automate the decision?

The last metric of supply chain visibility scorecard is simply the solution cost. This category could be expanded to offer a more subtle view on costs, such as direct operating costs vs. fixed asset costs. Unlike the first four metrics described above, the cost of a visibility solution doesn't connect to only one of its process steps but to the overall solution.

From Metrics to Fitness

The metrics described above help breakdown the visibility performance so that each process step can be measured. To be effective, the supply chain visibility scorecard provides three more tools:

1. Quantitative scales for the metrics.

2. Guidance on how to aggregate the individual metrics in to a single performance or fitness grade.

3. Methodology for how to conduct comparisons of multiple visibility options by using the scorecard.

Regarding the first point, an associated grading scale is described below for the first four metrics; with "cost" assumed to be standard enough it doesn't require a novel quantification approach. The grading scales are examined in detail in the following tables, while points two and three are addressed afterwards.

The scales provided may not be perfect, but they provide formal guidance about how to quantify what might otherwise be qualitatively graded. In particular, these scales are useful when teams of supply chain professionals must work together to evaluate, critique, or compare visibility solutions. In that sense any shortcomings in the proposed scales can be overcome by the team collectively agreeing on new grading guidelines. If it is agreed that visibility is better when it is highly sensitive, and that sensitivity should be quantifiable, the team can then promulgate and adopt guidelines on their grading approach as they see fit. The grading scale for decision relevance is perhaps the most robust because it has roots in human-systems interaction and design research (Parasuraman, Sheridan, and Wickens, 2000).

Table 2.1   Grading scale for supply chain visibility sensitivity

Score	Description
0	No data is captured to support the target business decision.
1	Some relevant data is captured, but it is incomplete.
2	All data is captured but the accuracy of the data is unknown or known to be low.
3	Data is complete and consistently biased (i.e. low quality but predictable).
4	All data needed to support the decision is captured, complete, consistent, and measurably high in accuracy.

Table 2.2   Grading scale for supply chain visibility accessibility

Score	Description
0	Data remains in the capturing systems with no attempt to integrate the data for later use.
1	Data remains in the capturing systems, but processes allow them to be manually integrated for ad-hoc tasks.
2	The solution integrates all the decision-relevant data, but not all of it is retrievable by decision makers.
3	Data is integrated and available to the decision maker, but not using the methods they prefer.
4	All relevant data is integrated and accessible by any relevant path the decision maker could use.
5	All relevant data is integrated, accessible, and the approach to integrating data is easily adapted.
6	All relevant data is integrated, accessible, and the integration approach is self-updating when confronting new data types or sources.

Table 2.3   Grading scale for supply chain visibility intelligence

Score	Description
0	There is no automated recognition from the solution that a business decision is needed.
1	Sometimes there is recognition from the solution that a business decision is needed.
2	The solution always knows that the business decision is needed.
3	The solution's approach to recognizing the need for a business decision is easily updated by users.
4	The solution's approach to recognizing the need for a business decision is self-updating.

Table 2.4   Grading scale for supply chain visibility decision relevance

Score	Description
0	The solution has no explicit input to this business decision.
1	The solution is a required information source for the decision maker. A user decides how and when to make the decision.
2	The solution is a required information source for the decision maker. The solution decides when the decision is taken and the user decides everything else.
3	The solution offers a set of action alternatives based on the event, or
4	narrows the selection down to a few, or
5	suggests one action, and
6	executes that suggestion if the human approves, or
7	allows the human a restricted time to veto before automatic execution, or
8	executes automatically, then necessarily informs the human, or
9	informs the human only if asked, or
10	The solution decides everything and acts autonomously, with no notice given to humans except for debugging.

Once a team accepts these grading scales or adopts their own, the next step is to agree on how the individual metric grades are combined to achieve an overall fitness score for the visibility process. Many projects to build or improve supply chain visibility get off-track because they focus on functionality as a *benefit in itself*. This is simply not an accurate understanding of why visibility adds value. Features of a visibility system or process are only valuable to the degree that they *fit into the targeted business decision*. As an example, if a visibility process delivers beautiful visualizations of the meta-data, such as by plotting flows of materials and capital onto a map, this is an interesting feature. But if the targeted business decisions don't have use for the feature, then it's not going to add value to the company. The degree to which a visibility process meets the targeted business needs is what is being labeled the "fitness," i.e. how good of a fit exists between the needs of the decision-making process and the output offered by the visibility process. On the high end would be a 100 percent fit, where the visibility solution literally fully automates the decision at or above levels possible by a human being. At the other end is zero percent fitness, where the system adds nothing meaningful to the decision-making process.

Later researchers may introduce more nuanced formula, but for now it's proposed to take a naïve view and assume that each of the four metric scores should simply be added and the sum divided by the maximum possible score so as to have the fitness percent score. Decision relevance is the most important metric, since it measures the most important step in the visibility process: decision interruption. But it doesn't seem necessary to add a weighting to this metric because the associated grading scale goes to 10 points compared to the others which go to four or six, so it is roughly double the value of any one of the other three metrics already. In short, it's suggested to use the grading scales to assign a score to each metric, then sum those scores and divide by 24. This gives a percentage of visibility fitness to the targeted business decision, indicating how well tuned the steps of the visibility process are compared to their ideal standards.

Ideally the scorecard could be used to compare visibility fitness across multiple solutions or options. This is where the cost metric comes in to play, as it factors in to the efficiency of the visibility process as a whole. What is suggested here is a specialized kind of cost-benefit analysis. From the total solution perspective, visibility efficiency would be the percentage of fitness achieved for a given investment by the company. When multiple options for how to deploy or improve supply chain visibility are available to a company, the company can evaluate the fitness percentage for each option and then plot fitness against cost to identify the efficiency frontier. This approach draws on non-parametric data envelopment analysis techniques, but the output is extremely easy to understand even by persons not directly or deeply involved in the evaluation. As an example, here is a fictive case study which traces ten visibility options as they are graded at the process-step level, then for overall fitness, and finally contrasted against one another in terms of efficiency.

Table 2.5a   Example scorecarding of ten visibility solutions

Solution	Sensitivity	Accessibility	Intelligence	Decision Relevance
A	2	2	3	1
B	3	5	0	5
C	1	3	2	3
D	2	4	2	4
E	3	5	2	3
F	4	2	1	5
G	2	2	3	2
H	2	5	3	2
I	4	4	0	2
J	3	3	2	3
K	3	3	1	2

Table 2.5b   Example fitness percent of the ten visibility solutions

Solution	Sensitivity	Accessibility	Intelligence	Decision Relevance	Fitness
A	2	2	3	1	33%
B	3	5	0	5	54%
C	1	3	2	3	38%
D	2	4	2	4	50%
E	3	5	2	3	54%
F	4	2	1	5	50%
G	2	2	3	2	38%
H	1	4	3	2	50%
I	4	4	0	2	42%
J	3	3	2	3	46%
K	3	3	1	2	38%

Table 2.5c   Fitness and cost of the ten visibility solutions

Solution	Sensitivity	Accessibility	Intelligence	Decision Relevance	Fitness	Solution Cost in Thousands of USD
A	2	2	3	1	33%	850
B	3	5	0	5	54%	1,120
C	1	3	2	3	38%	775
D	2	4	2	4	50%	915
E	3	5	2	3	54%	1,300
F	4	2	1	5	50%	1,050
G	2	2	3	2	38%	925
H	2	5	3	2	50%	890
I	4	4	0	2	42%	790
J	3	3	2	3	46%	860
K	3	3	1	2	38%	900

The last table shows how the ten visibility options create a best-tradeoff frontier regarding fitness and cost, also known as the efficiency frontier. Obviously it is of limited use to compare high and low cost options in terms of cost alone. But this graphic and the associated approach allows for a simple and visual display of tradeoffs which occur between cost and visibility fitness. The dashed line shows the efficiency frontier (a concept borrowed from the data envelopment analysis domain). Solution options on this frontier represent

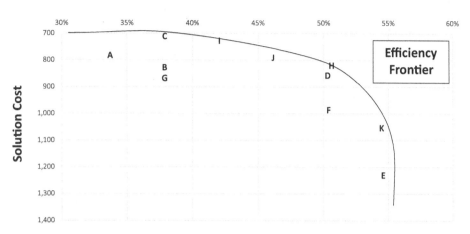

·Figure 2.8   The efficiency frontier for visibility solutions

the best tradeoff between cost and visibility fitness. Solution options which are enveloped by this line are not as efficient, and hence they should not be considered further. Another way to say this is that the solution options not on the frontier will always be dominated by another option. In this example, option B shows such domination. For the same cost, one could go with option H and have higher visibility fitness. Alternatively, one could achieve the same fitness as option B but at a lower cost by selecting option C. In either dimension (cost or fitness) the option B is dominated by another solution, therefore it should never be selected. Although this same measurement (fitness/cost) can be shown in a tabular view, the graphical view is simple to make and easy for decision makers, stakeholders, or other interested parties to understand. It goes a long way towards depoliticizing the removal of certain visibility options during real projects. But in most situations there will still be multiple solutions which form the fitness-cost frontier, and then it's a question of organizational priorities to decide what level of cost and fitness is right for the company. This is valuable because it converts the problem of evaluating differing visibility solutions from a puzzle, dilemma, or paradox into a tradeoff. See the Figure 2.9 on the following page, derived from work on problems as strategic tensions in organizations (De Wit and Meyer, 2005), for a comparison on how these kinds of problems are evaluated. By reclassifying the problem as such, it (a) eliminates dominated solutions and (b) allows the organization to have fruitful discussions on where they should be on the tradeoff line, while knowing there is fundamentally no perfect answer to a tradeoff problem.

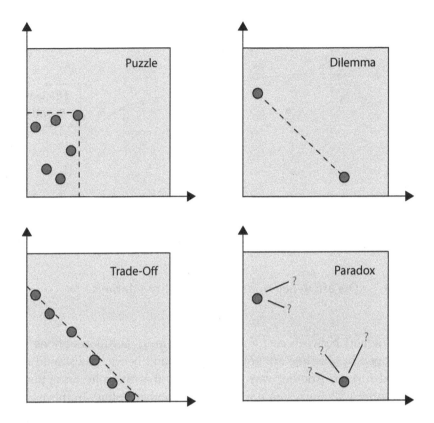

Figure 2.9   Problem typologies: Puzzles, dilemmas, paradoxes, and tradeoffs

Procedurally, this is the suggested way to use the supply chain visibility fitness scorecard. First, list the targeted business decisions which the visibility solution or solutions should support. If multiple visibility solutions are being compared they must be targeting the same business decisions. Otherwise comparisons are not informative, in the sense that the "appleness of an orange" or "orangeness of an apple" is not informative. The figure opposite shows a mocked up scorecard where the evaluator or evaluation team can list out the decisions being targeted in the column on the far left. Just listing those decisions (and agreeing on them among the group involved) should drive the process towards better results because it focuses on the expected impact of the visibility rather than the visibility features in isolation. As one practitioner interviewee put it: "Supply chain visibility is a means, not an end. You must define what you are trying to achieve within the organization and how supply chain visibility can play a role" (Wilkie, Appendix A). Create one of these pages for each visibility option being evaluated, but as described previously they must be evaluated

Supply Chain Visibility Scorecard

Visibility Solution Name: _____

Business Decision	Sensitivity	Accessibility	Intelligence	Decision-Relevance	Fit %

Estimated Total Cost: _____   Overall Fit %: _____

Figure 2.10   The supply chain visibility scorecard

based on the same targeted decisions. At the bottom of the page is a field for the total cost of this solution, and the overall fitness score. Using one sheet per solution, evaluate the four metrics for each decision and then add their scores and divide by 24 to get the fitness percentage and place it in the column on the far right. After all options are evaluated this way, plot the solutions in terms of overall fitness percent on one axis and the cost of the solution on the other axis. Finally, draw a line to indicate the efficiency frontier, and then eliminate any solutions not on the frontier. Those options which remain can only be selected in terms of organizational priorities, as they represent the best possible tradeoff in terms of effectiveness for the investment at different investment levels.

To summarize, the supply chain visibility scorecard is a novel framework for evaluating the effectiveness of supply chain visibility, including the four steps in the visibility process. It fills an important area of assessment which has not been well studied up to now in the theory of supply chain visibility. It also has the benefit of providing decomposed metrics that align to the supply chain visibility process steps, which supports fine tuning of existing or proposed visibility solutions because the evaluator knows what part of the visibility process is contributing to a higher or lower fitness score. In the presence of multiple visibility solutions, or possible variations on a single solution, evaluators can introduce the dimension of total solution cost and compare it to the visibility fitness percentage in order to remove dominated options. In particular, this is useful during technology or strategic partner selection processes or periodic supply chain improvement projects. By adopting the data envelopment analysis methodology of plotting the fitness compared to the cost, an easily understood graph is available to share with colleagues, which tends to increase transparency about why certain options are favored over others. In a concise format, the steps to using the visibility scorecard are described below. See also Appendix B for a three-page evaluation instrument made from this methodology.

Steps to Use the Supply Chain Visibility Scorecard

1. For each visibility solution option, create a scorecard.

2. Add the list of business decisions which should be improved by supply chain visibility, and ensure the decisions listed are the same for all options being evaluated.

3. After studying the solution design, and using the grading guidelines provided, give each business decision a score for each

category. The grading guide can be changed to provide more or less weight on certain areas, as long as the same guidelines are used by all evaluators and for all solution options.

4. Sum the scores by business decision and divide the sum by 24. This is the "fitness" for the solution compared to the ideal support for the business decision.

5. Average the decision fitness percentages and add to the solution the expected costs.

6. Plot the relationship between fitness percentage and solution costs and then eliminate any options which are strongly dominated by the efficiency frontier.

7. The remaining options represent the frontier of tradeoffs between fitness and the solution cost. Differentiating between these options requires assessing the organizations priorities.

Before closing the topic of the supply chain visibility scorecard, we should note that any visibility project can have external considerations in addition to the fitness to cost ratio. For example, there may be two visibility solutions under consideration for a company, but one of the options involves an external provider with bad financial health. The risk that the partner goes bankrupt and stops the project is *not* included in the visibility scorecard. This doesn't mean that the financial health of the provider isn't important, it just means that the scorecard is only targeted as specific visibility results achieved by the visibility solution. Professionals who are steering key visibility projects in their organizations can and should continue to look at the larger business environment for risks, synergies, conflicts of interests, and so forth.

PART 2
Supply Chain Visibility in Practice

3

Popular Types of Visibility

There are so many flavors of supply chain visibility that at times it can seem we are in error to group them together. Several practitioner interviewees spoke of the duality in visibility solutions, that they are unique in implementation but consistent in principles (see Appendix A for full transcripts). As an example, one interviewee noted:

> There is also the important differentiation, even within an industry, of how each company tries to position itself against the competition. Cost-leaders will approach visibility completely differently from a fashion or service leader, for example (Karel, Appendix A).

This chapter reviews popular visibility setups. It is not an exhaustive list, but understanding how and why these types of visibility are popular teaches a lot about other variations and arms new practitioners with a broader set of templates for how visibility can be achieved. We'll look at eight types of supply chain visibility in depth:

1. Classic Track and Trace: Inbound to Retailers.

2. World as a Warehouse.

3. The Event Manager: Managing by Exception.

4. Mobile Decision Making with GPS and Visibility.

5. Save the Sale: Extended Enterprise Visibility for Retailers.

6. Lot and Serial Number Tracking.

7. Competitive Landscape and Market Visibility.

8.   Inventory Visibility.

Classic Track and Trace: Inbound to Retailers

This is probably the most common visibility setup in the retail industry in North America. It is less popular in other geographic markets because it assumes:

1.   A long lead-time between supplier ex-factory date and availability date on the retailer shelf; and

2.   Assumes no middlemen wholesalers or distributors between the supplier and the retailer.

Both of these conditions are realistic for medium and large-sized retailers in North America, but less so for retailers in other markets. In the rest of the discussion we assume the following are involved:

- A retailer who imports merchandise.

- Suppliers in Asia sending product to North America.

- Product lifecycles that necessitate launch-and-retire activities.

Retailers of high margin items are continuously preparing for a new product launch. This could be a seasonal launch (Valentine's Day, for example), a new product line (iPhone 4G), a public event (movie premier featuring new Ray-Ban glasses), and so forth. The retailer has a number of business decisions that can be greatly improved by visibility to what is in transit and when it is expected to arrive.

If these decisions are repeated continuously, such as every four weeks with a monthly product release, they have a combined major financial impact on the company. For a publicly listed company in the USA, we'd be able to see impacts on:

- Return on Assets (ROA) or its cousin Economic Value-Add (EVA).

- Inventory turn ratio.

- Sell-through rates.

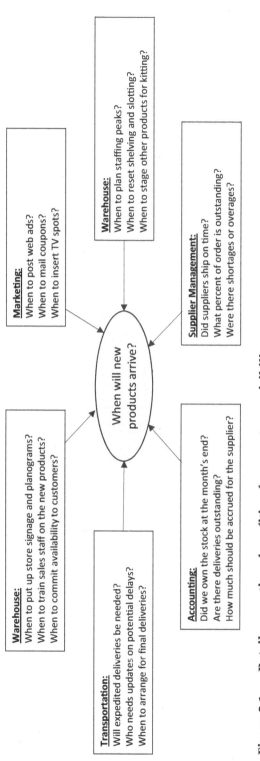

Warehouse:
When to put up store signage and planograms?
When to train sales staff on the new products?
When to commit availability to customers?

Transportation:
Will expedited deliveries be needed?
Who needs updates on potential delays?
When to arrange for final deliveries?

Marketing:
When to post web ads?
When to mail coupons?
When to insert TV spots?

When will new products arrive?

Warehouse:
When to plan staffing peaks?
When to reset shelving and slotting?
When to stage other products for kitting?

Accounting:
Did we own the stock at the month's end?
Are there deliveries outstanding?
How much should be accrued for the supplier?

Supplier Management:
Did suppliers ship on time?
What percent of order is outstanding?
Were there shortages or overages?

Figure 3.1 Retailer questions benefiting from upstream visibility

- Inventory restatement frequency, after closing months or quarters.

- Labor or staffing costs.

- Operations costs.

- Gross Margin (GM).

This kind of supply chain visibility is commonly achieved through very basic initiatives. In reality, most retailers achieve this level of supply chain visibility without a specific IT application assigned to the solution. By combining existing tools, like email, Excel, and 3PL track and trace websites, small to medium-sized retailers can go far into this kind of visibility without a direct IT investment. Most solutions will use a high-level process that involves these steps:

1. Capture the end-of-production Work in Progress (WIP) events.

2. Capture the contents of shipments leaving the supplier.

3. Match shipment events to the shipment contents.

4. Use the shipment content and transport events to create forecasted delivery dates for specific items, POs, locations, and so forth.

5. Publish the forecasts to decision makers.

The five steps above are generalized of course, but they are present in nearly all the solutions to the business problem of upstream shipment visibility for retailers. Here are those steps again but with more details added:

1st – CAPTURE THE END-OF-PRODUCTION WORK IN PROGRESS (WIP) EVENTS

As the supplier nears the completion of their production schedule, the retailer will expect some kind of signal to indicate the production status. This can be low-tech, such as a telephone call or email. It can be consistent or only for special orders. It can be direct or via an agent. The point of the step is to be able to confirm actual status since it often differs from the requested or planned schedule.

2ND – CAPTURE THE CONTENTS OF SHIPMENTS

In reality, only the supplier knows what they pack into a shipment. In some situations, the supplier doesn't even know their own shipment contents with high accuracy. Retailers facing this upstream visibility problem will ask suppliers for shipment content details. This can be an Excel spreadsheet, an ASN, an EDI transmission, or even a fax of the packing list. By knowing what products are packed into each shipment, the retailer enables their decision makers to take actions later at the shipment-level (such as prioritization of delivery sequence) when what they really care about is the products those shipments contain.

3RD – MATCH SHIPMENT EVENTS TO SHIPMENT CONTENTS

Transporters will not generally know what is in a sealed container, truck, or pallet. But they can be made to report events to the retailer at the level of the shipment. For example, they may inform the retailer that pallet #1234 was delayed on its departure from an air freight hub. The retailer is usually responsible for connecting the event from the shipment-level back to product on the shipment. Alternatively, 3PLs provide this connection as a service, using their visibility tools.

4TH – CREATE OR UPDATE PRODUCT-AVAILABILITY FORECASTS

The retailer (or sometimes the 3PL) will take the information about shipment contents, and shipment milestones, along with other information, and produce product-level forecasts. This process can be very simple or rather complex. For example, analysts may use historical data about transport timeliness and warehouse processing times to make their estimates. They may also plan for selected or random QA holds. On the simpler end of the spectrum of practices, the retailer may just take the expected delivery date and add an arbitrary number (say two days) as the estimate for availability. Weather, working hours, upcoming holidays, and other factors can be used in this process.

5TH – PUBLISH FORECASTS TO DECISION MAKERS

The last step, and often the place where these visibility solutions fail, is the publishing of product availability forecasts to decision makers. This can be done through scheduled publications (every Monday, for example), through on-demand publishing, or through alerts. Questions of timeliness, consistency, usability, and user trust are all given attention in this step. For companies with low-level visibility capabilities, the publishing is almost informal and prone to be poorly integrated with decision making. Organizations with mature visibility practices will have fully integrated decision support from the forecasts, perhaps including monitoring of the decision outcome compared to the forecast inputs. As an example, a warehouse manager may be reviewed by her boss by comparing her receiving-dock labor overtime as to delivery forecast accuracy. If delivery forecast accuracy is high, the receiving labor overtime would be expected to be minimal.

In summary, the "classic track and trace" model is about feeding forecasts of inbound merchandise availability to the retailer's decision makers so they can improve overall sales performance. This is, by far, the most common kind of visibility being rolled out to retailers in North America. It is low risk, low cost, requires no direct IT investment, and is somewhat self-organizing. Left alone, most retailers will evolve some version of this visibility because it is so obviously beneficial and easy to put in place. Ironically, the fact that it evolves naturally tends to make it hard to replace a mediocre setup with a really good setup. The benefits and responsibilities are too dispersed, and the stakeholder list is quite large. It is not unusual for each department to have similar but different merchandise availability estimates being used by their decision makers.

World as a Warehouse

Large supply chains cover many different places, people, and processes. Although a factory in Brazil and a factory in China may produce the same SKU, everything about the two sites is subtly different and the supply chain manager's life is often caught up in dealing with those inconsistencies. And the number and consequences of inconsistencies grows when we look across hundreds of sites and tens of thousands of products and dozens of channels to market. How can the supply chain managers control such diverse, decentralized, and partially synchronized operations? One approach is to use a visibility layer to approximate a planet-wide warehouse: total control and traceability of materials at any physical point on the earth, using a common architecture and process.

In long or interconnecting channels to market the materials tend to move through various independent locations, often at great distances apart, before reaching end customers. For example, consider a company which produces laptops, sells them direct to customers, and then delivers to the consumer's home or office. The expensive and rapidly obsolete parts may be built in Taiwan and air freighted to Germany and then sent via truck to Poland. The more basic parts which are not at risk to become obsolete are produced in China and shipped via ocean freight to Rotterdam, then railed to Poland. Finally, the heavy and low-value packaging and instruction manuals are printed in Poland locally. As web orders come in, the Polish assembly factory combines materials to create a custom laptop. The orders are bundled, then consolidated based on delivery region, and packed onto trucks by the end of the day. The transit to final delivery may be two to three days, during which time the boxed-up laptops get variously deconsolidated, sorted, reconsolidated, and trucked again. Finally the laptop is delivered. This is hardly an unusual example, so we see that even this basic supply chain involves:

- A lot of materials of various types, including finished and unfinished goods.

- Many independent organizations who manage, conduct work with, or are exchanging ownership of the supply chain's materials.

- Timelines in various material streams which must be closely synchronized.

- Goods which are valuable enough to track at the individual piece level.

- Language, working time zone, and business culture barriers.

A supply chain manager in this situation needs to know that each site (factory, cross-dock DC, warehouse, assembly factory, and transport depot) and each transporter (airlines, trucking companies, railroad companies, shipping lines) is making a handover of materials as expected. Note that the supply chain manager should not be thought of as sitting in some *central organization* (like the assembly factory in Poland). In reality, *every single organization* in this supply chain will employ someone to do supply chain management, and unless their available information is the same they will tend to make conflicting decisions. It's in everyone's interest that the status of the material flows are generally known, rather than only known by one central organization.

Of course there are more dimensions to the supply chain than just *material flow*, but it is a significant part of the supply chain management staff's daily work. The supply chain manager is constantly trying to capture, integrate, and disseminate material flow status out to other decision makers. This is how the optimal material flow (or any flow, really) gets achieved. To be specific, consider what happens when the coordinated flow of materials begins to deteriorate. There are classic case studies on companies that permanently lost market share or even ceased to survive as a result of these issues. Consider these examples:

- HP losing market share against Dell due to consistently holding more inventories when a technology component (like a processor) became obsolete.

- Zara exploding in Europe via its powerful and agile supply chain, only to stagnate in new markets when the supply chain could not deliver the same material flow in far-flung locations.

- Grocery stores losing revenue at Halloween when their candy supplier Hershey's misses key production and shipping timelines.

The defining aspect of this business problem also indicates the kind of solution the supply chain management team is looking for. The management team is usually talking about *material flow*, and the need to control and report on materials in terms of total quantity, status, location, and ownership. On smaller scales, these are the basis for a warehouse management system (WMS). For a WMS, the absolute minimum requirement is to track inventory of materials. Everything above the inventory tracking is important, but without inventory control no WMS would be viable.

Now take the WMS concept and push it outward so it covers more than one physical site. This is sometimes called "the warehouse without walls," "extended warehouse," and several other variations. The idea is that the same basic controls we want in a DC are made to cover multiple sites. In this book it's being labeled the "World as a Warehouse" type of supply chain visibility. When asked to describe how his company approached offering supply chain visibility, this is very close to the conceptual model described by some of the practitioner interviewees (Lienhard, Appendix A). In descending order of importance, the top three expectations on the visibility solution would look like:

1.   *Track all materials in the supply chain*: in terms of quantity, ownership, availability status, and location.

2. *Provide System Stand-In*: so all participant organizations have access to a "minimum capabilities" application, where they can keep the material tracking intact even if their physical site doesn't have its own IT system.

3. *Support Data Discovery*: Users should be able to find data they need from various angles (location, material ID, material attributes, company involved, and so forth).

Of the top three solution components, the only one that might need additional description is number two; the need for "system stand-in." The reality is that many physical sites either lack comprehensive material control systems, or those systems will prove incompatible with the targeted visibility needs. Here are two quick examples. First, consider a small hub where materials are deconsolidated for final delivery. This site may not have its own ERP or WMS. So, the visibility layer is expected to provide the hub with some minimal functionality to record material receipt, status updates, and outbound shipping. The "system stand-in" enables any site with web access (and even some without, if there is a batch option) to be covered in the "world as a warehouse" visibility solution.

The second example would be a site, like a major airport, where systems exist but are so different from the visibility needs that they cannot be effectively integrated. In these situations most companies go back to having a user access a web portal and "key in" the data. Although it sounds like a waste of human labor this may not be a double-entry of data because the site's system may not have the required data to begin with since it is so differently focused than the visibility solution. Nonetheless, having a user go to a web portal to key in data does introduce human error, timeliness issues, and generally feels like a work-around.

Of course, many visibility solutions that cater to the "world as a warehouse" type of visibility will offer more than just the three functionalities described above. They may also incorporate orders or sales, forecasts or plans, capacity or operating schedules, or invoice and reconciliation data. These are all great expansions on the tracking of material flow. But, as mentioned earlier, they come *after* the core needs are covered by the three requirements of material tracking, system stand-in, and easy data discovery.

In summary, there exists a certain type of supply chain visibility which is most successful when it delivers the functionality to treat all of the supply chain operations as a kind of planet-wide warehouse. Material flows tend to be more important (and difficult) to manage as they get longer, have more paths to market, must move faster, increase in value, increase in government oversight, or involve other merging material flows. So this type of visibility is attractive to larger organizations and less attractive to smaller organizations with simpler supply chains. When business problems are described primarily in terms of material flow and the lack of knowledge or certainty that the material flow is occurring as needed, this is a good indicator that the "world as a warehouse" type of visibility is a viable solution approach. It's also relatively simple to check if this type of visibility matches the business needs by imagining the improvements possible if all the supply chain occurred in one building, with one WMS running it all. If that idea doesn't appear to relieve the problems, then the "world as a warehouse" model isn't a good fit. For any visibility solution to meet the "world as a warehouse" model, it must provide at least these three points:

- Tracking of materials in terms of ownership, quantity, status, and location.

- Easy to use, easy to learn, low-risk tools which can be engaged optionally as a system stand-in if a site in the supply chain can't provide the necessary data via integration.

- Appropriate data discovery and escape paths for getting key data out of the visibility application and into another form needed for decisions.

Finally, the "world as a warehouse" type of visibility is a very logistics-oriented way of looking at the supply chain. As a result, these projects tend to be easier to implement because they have less departmental stakeholders and a simpler scope of what is being managed (materials).

The Event Manager: Managing by Exception

The phrase "manage by exception" pretty well summarizes the driving spirit behind event management as a kind of supply chain visibility. There is a separate literature about supply chain event management, but when it's cross-organizational it can also be considered as a variant of supply chain visibility. A recent analyst review of supply chain visibility technology identified event management type visibility as the most impactful (Cap Gemini, 2012). This type of visibility is particularly valuable for supply chains with two specific attributes:

- Supply chain sourcing, production, and distribution plans with little slack between the planned activities.

- Downstream commitments or requirements where fast and pro-active management is valuable.

As an example, consider a watch company that contracts the production of its components, the assembly operation, and then transports and distributes the watches to department stores and boutiques. Given the cost of a high-end watch, its relative low volume of units sold, and the risk of theft, most retailers will want to hold a very minimal stock level. This puts pressure on the watch company to either hold stock in its own DC or to have a very responsive supply chain. Let's assume the watch company decides to make the assembly flexible and to execute it at the last minute, when actual demand is known. Every event during the sourcing of raw materials and production of the components has ripple effects down through the assembly plan, the transport and distribution plan, and the ability to commit to sales and even marketing for related products. Because components can be used for multiple final watches (think about the watch hand, which may be the same for dozens of different watches), the effect of one change to the production plan is unpredictable on the downstream plans. The same is true for the relationship between raw materials and the components, where the delay of one raw material (like a specific grade of crystal watch cover) causes multiple components to be re-planned, which in turn causes multiple watches to be re-planned for assembly: onward and onward through the cascading supply chain plans. There are literally thousands of individual SKU-plans being managed at any time, most of them interconnected and sensitive to deviation events in their predecessors or successors. So, one can see the kind of pressure which leads to event management as a kind of supply chain visibility.

In the "event manager" type of supply chain visibility a system acts as an ever-constant watchmen over the supply chain. In the simplest visibility setups of this kind, the visibility comes from watching for *status changes* of important objects, like shipments or orders. More complex setups watch for pre-defined events outside of just status. They may look at variables like quantity, expected event dates for planned activities, or calculated values like maximum possible counterparty credit risk. Finally, very advanced event management visibility includes a machine learning component where the events are not always explicitly defined, but instead an application or system develops event definitions in reaction to the data and feedback it receives.

Supply chain visibility focused on event management is valuable to the extent that it does these things. Note the congruity between these value-adding aspects of event management and the visibility scorecard categories:

- Reduces labor or cost required to identify an event has occurred.

- Compresses the time taken for follow-up actions after an event.

- Improves the quality of event identification or follow-up actions.

- Reduces the labor or cost required to take follow up actions.

Of the four value-adding aspects above, three are focused on the actions taken as a result of an event occurring. So it's no surprise that the event management type of supply chain visibility usually involves partially or fully automated actions tied to defined events. Simpler setups use the event as a trigger for an email notification. More complex setups have decision trees where the action taken is dependent not just on the event itself but on other environmental factors. Fully automated systems cover most appropriate post-event actions in a way that is as good as or better than human staff could achieve.

In summary, the "event manager" type of supply chain visibility tries to support supply chain wide, near real-time planning and re-planning based on events as they occur. Because of its focus on events and particularly events which will cause knock-on effects to other supply chain plans, this type of supply chain visibility is seen mostly in large manufacturing companies. These companies might at first seem like good candidates for the "world as a warehouse" type of supply chain. And, of course, they might benefit from that model as well. But more likely they are looking to use visibility for planned or unplanned events to reconfigure downstream activities. That focus on timely visibility as a means to better downstream planning is the defining characteristic of the event manager type of visibility.

Mobile Decision Making with GPS and Visibility

The web 2.0 catchphrase "mashup" refers to the ability to integrate heterogeneous data sources into a single, consistent view for greater total value to the user. Mashups, both useful and dubious, are making their way into supply chain visibility toolsets. One type of supply chain visibility focuses on the productive mashup between supply chain data and GPS location devices riding with delivery drivers. In this context geospatial data is actually much easier to use than we might expect. In the end, this type of supply chain visibility is an example of "simple solutions to complex problems."

The first type of supply chain visibility discussed in this chapter (classic track and trace: inbound to retailer) is most commonly seen with North American retailers. The type of visibility described below is the opposite: it is predominate among direct-to-consumer manufacturing, oil and gas service and spare part logistics, driver-managed-inventory, and in countries with fast growing and somewhat disorganized public road networks. The reason that this type of visibility is more common for these sectors and geographies is that the visibility solution acts as a quality assurance technique for enforcing that a transaction takes place at a specified geographic point. It will be more valuable to industries that deliver to dynamically changing locations, to locations that are remote and expensive to find, and where there isn't an easy-to-use street address (such as finding an off-shore oil rig, where there is no street address).

As an example, consider a manufacturer who sells refrigerators direct to customer in remote areas of China. They employ local traveling sales representatives who go door-to-door looking for customers. When a sale is agreed, the manufacturer arranges direct delivery to the customer's home a week later. The salesperson is not responsible for delivery, so the delivery driver will go to make the drop-off alone. The business problem with these deliveries is that the public road network is underdeveloped in tier three communities in China, and the refrigerator can easily be "lost." In practice the term "lost" is used to mean that a mistaken address and wrong delivery is practically impossible to correct. The accidental recipient will refuse to return the new, expensive item they received. Therefore, the company has to achieve verification of the delivery addresses to a high quality standard before they complete the delivery. Remember, the potential address format for a place like this is *not* consistent, and that there is no central database to validate against. Finally, delays and mis-delivery events generate overhead costs in dealing with the customer, the transportation staff, and the loss of brand equity.

The traditional (and wrong) way to resolve the problem would be to form centralized databases on "correct" addresses. Then, orders would be validated against the database. Finally, the address data would drive load and route planning for outbound vehicles. But, of course, this is nonsense outside of a few specific countries. In the USA it works well, in the UK it works for some but not all areas (Northern Ireland still has roads with no name or numbers). The Chinese government doesn't publish (or even allow others to publish) comprehensive address databases. And any attempt to do so would be silly, given the incredible volume of changes occurring in the country's road network. Every year, China adds more road kilometers than all of France's road network combined. Whole cities are being relocated, and construction of new buildings (hence addresses) usually occurs in parallel with a change in the local road and address format.

Quite simply, the best solution to this problem comes from not relying on the street address at all and switching to the GPS coordinates. Where an address can be wrong or misread, it is practically impossible to have an incorrect GPS coordinate. Of course, the salesperson could mis-key the GPS coordinates. So, rather than key it in manually the sales person carries a GPS-enabled mobile device which is used to register the order. At the time the order is confirmed, the GPS coordinates are loaded into the order database. The next logical step is to do the GPS check automatically, rather than with the driver's eyes. To accomplish this, the driver also carries a GPS-enabled mobile device. The driver's device software checks its present coordinates against the order's delivery coordinates. Until the driver is within a specific range, the order cannot be released. In other words, the driver cannot capture a proof of delivery signature until they are within a specific radius of the expected coordinates for delivery. This is a simple and proven technique to minimize incorrect deliveries and their associated costs.

The example above involves a manufacturer who sells direct to consumers. Another frequent place to find GPS-enabled supply chain visibility is in the oil and gas sector, where engineers take spare parts out to remote locations to conduct testing and repairs. In these situations there can be large financial loss if the engineer conducts work at the wrong location. For example, if they conduct repairs on one oil rig but should have worked on another one five hundred meters away. Most of these kinds of industrial sites don't have formal addresses, street signs, or street numbers. Even if an offshore oil platform had a street address like "1212 Deep-Water Drive," that address may not help a lost engineer because it doesn't indicate in which direction the correct site is at (i.e. are the street numbers going up or down). By enabling their handheld devices with GPS coordinates, the engineer can confirm a site, but also more easily find the location to begin with. One aspect of this type of supply chain visibility which is interesting is that it is more of a local than a global solution.

In most visibility setups, the goal is to achieve central and uniform visibility functionality. In the GPS-enabled mobile decision-making kind of visibility the focus is on making better decisions locally. Nothing about the decision-making process is improved by extending the scope of visibility larger than the local needs.

In summary, this type of visibility is predominate in industries where deliveries are made to remote, difficult to access, or unverifiable addresses. It is a good fit for countries where a single database of valid addresses, along with directions of how to get there, is not available or realistic to create. Finally, this kind of supply chain visibility is more valuable when the act of delivery is itself difficult to reverse or expensive to fix if done incorrectly. For these reasons just listed we tend to see supply chain visibility focused on GPS integration in the oil and gas sector or direct-to-consumer manufacturing and driver managed inventory models for the consumer goods sector. Although the GPS-enabled hand held device might seem complicated to integrate, in reality this is a fairly simple kind of supply chain visibility. It nicely and deeply interrupts the driver's decision-making process for different and better outcomes.

Save the Sale: Extended-Enterprise Visibility for Retailers

Retailers hate the idea of losing a sale. Those practitioners who work or have worked in the retail sector know that there is extreme attention given to the conversion process between making the consumer aware that a retailer exists, getting them to the point of sale (website or store or kiosk, etc.), getting them to select a product, and then getting that shopping cart converted to a payment. At each step there are a portion of consumers who simply abandon the process. How can visibility help increase conversion and save sales? For some of the failed conversions, retailers lose the potential sales because they have the capacity to fulfill the demand but not at the point of sale the customer is attempting to use. Take for example a customer who is at a store in a mall in the UK and has asked for item XYZ, but that item is out of stock in the store. Traditionally this is simply a lost sale: the customer is leaving empty handed (barring a clever salesperson who is able to direct them to a product substitution). But with the right visibility tools, the salesperson can also commit to the customer to get the product from somewhere in the company network within a short period of time. As the customer starts to walk out the door the store clerk says "wait one second, I'll check if it can be delivered tomorrow and we'll give you a ten percent discount for the delay." This is what is meant by "save the sale," and this kind of visibility appears in some of the interviews with industry practitioners (Wilkie, Appendix A). Without visibility, it could never be done at the enterprise scale and in the time a customer is willing to stand and wait in the store.

It's important to understand all the business impacts a lost sale will cause. Obviously it has an immediate impact of lowering revenue. But, beneath this effect, there are a few others. Retailers are notoriously ill-equipped to capture statistics on unsatisfied demand. That is to say, when this sales opportunity is lost the retailer probably also ends up with a distorted view of true customer demand because they won't have recorded the lost sale. Next season, the retailer may choose the wrong product line-up, not realizing a best-seller had been sidetracked by product being in the wrong place. Revenue is important, but accurate demand insight is critical for managing higher-margin products. Besides a distorted picture of demand, the retailer is losing brand equity. Getting customers into the store usually involves some kind of promise, for example through advertising the latest styles. If a customer arrives and that promise is not fulfilled, the respect for the brand is hurt.

In order to "save the sale," visibility systems will try to provide as much inventory and capacity summary and commitment capabilities as possible into a very fast interface for the retail staff. How the visibility system does this largely depends on the supply chain and retail channel in question. To keep things simple we'll look at three different retail networks: clustered bricks and mortar stores, e-commerce, and multi-channel. We'll now look at these three in turn.

In retailers where stores are clustered into an urban area or region, the "save the sale" visibility solution is commonly a virtual-warehouse which wraps around all the nearby inventory pools. For example, the Starbucks strategy of saturating urban markets means they have many stores holding stock near to each other. By combining their inventory into a virtual pool the stores are able to carry lower individual stock levels on things like French coffee presses while knowing that if one store has high demand the other nearby stores can make same day or next day transfers to them to avoid stock outs. Without a visibility solution along these lines, when a single Starbucks runs out of stock on an item then customer sales are refused or delayed until the item is back in stock, regardless of how many units could be shipped from all the other nearby stores. The visibility solutions also usually encompass shipments inbound from the warehouse so that the inventory picture is complete. From a usability perspective, these visibility solutions are accessed by store staff and can directly initiate a diversion, a lock on inventory, or a request to nearby stores. These visibility practices are purely to support making commitments to customers, not as a means to make normal replenishment orders.

During the rise of e-retailing it was common for sales to be supported out of a single bricks and mortar store. But, of course, the growth of web sales caused a migration to large-scale web fulfillment centers. These sites deal with orders in a production-line process, which improves labor efficiency. But things are changing again. The current trend is for supply chain leaders to look more closely at inventory and capacity smoothing when sales can only be processed by one or two web centers. Visibility solutions for "save the sale" in e-commerce are focused on allowing orders to be fulfilled from alternate locations (i.e. not the main processing centers) when they would have to otherwise be refused due to inventory or capacity limits. For example, if a customer is online and orders item ABC the shopping cart application first checks the inventory at the company's main web fulfillment center. If the item is out of stock, the web cart does a look-up to find the item in other, less labor-efficient locations. The business rules for where it can look are part of the visibility solution's design. Unlike the bricks and mortar example above, an e-commerce visibility solution to "save the sale" is going to have to be very, *very* fast. The norm might be a one to two second delay between when the user clicks "Purchase" and when the website responds with a confirmation on inventory availability and expected delivery date. Accounting for other tasks and internet latency, the visibility system will need to provide sub-second inventory search and reservation. And unlike the bricks and mortar example, the visibility solution is directly responsible for deciding the ordering, inventory lock, or inventory diversion actions necessary to meet those commitments. It is not just a tool but also a decision maker. Whereas the bricks and mortar example would include shipments in-transit; most e-commerce "save the sale" type visibility will not take into consideration inventory that is in a shipment which is inbound to one of the valid processing centers.

Very similar in nature to e-commerce is the rise of multi-channel demand and visibility systems to help "save the sale" in these formats. Multi-channel demand is manifested when the customer is actively shopping through more than one point of sale. They may shop online and then buy in-store, browse in-store and order over the phone, or order online and arrange for pickup at a store, and so forth. Visibility solutions that try to "save the sale" for multi-channel supply chains will offer transparency of inventory and availability for the customer, but also try to provide the retailer with transparency to the real customer interaction lifecycle. In the e-commerce example, the inventory visibility and procurement or diversion of stock was masked from the final customer. For example, when they order a pair of high-end shoes from a website, the website isn't going to make them read through its process of finding the right inventory and assigning a picking task. But, in a multi-channel situation, the real goal of the visibility solution might be to demonstrate the multi-channel options to the customer during the sales process. As an example, when a customer is looking at renting a tuxedo the retailer will attempt to "save the sale" by having an improved inventory visibility for the customer to use directly. The customer can then see what styles and sizes are available immediately via different channels, and (the retailer hopes) this results in a higher conversion rate. In multi-channel markets, the customer was already active in several points of sale. By using a supply chain visibility application to tie the points of sale together into one experience, the retailer delivers higher total service. This type of visibility is also good at connecting what would otherwise be distinct events at different consumer-retailer touch points. For example, the multi-channel retailer needs to know what proportion of its in-store sales began as web experiences, and vice-versa. Visibility solutions to "save the sale" in multichannel operations will often be designed to capture that kind of channel-hopping statistic.

Another type of visibility is discussed later in the book, that of inventory visibility. A fair question might be "what makes save-the-sale a different type of visibility and not just a usage-case for inventory visibility"? The answer is that the need to save a sale, a single unique sale, tends to lead to a very different visibility system and associated process. For example, the need to interrupt a failing sale on an e-commerce site requires extremely low latency systems, which is not a common feature of inventory visibility or other types of visibility listed in this book. When making sourcing decisions or product distribution decisions, it's okay to spend several minutes optimizing an inventory placement. But this timescale is totally unacceptable for e-commerce customers who want sub-second confirmation when they interact with a website.

In summary, the "save the sale" type of visibility is designed to maximize the usability of the retailer's supply chain data when making goods available to promise even if the transaction must be delayed, altered, or moved to a different point of sale. It comes from a desire to "save a sale" by having a more complete knowledge of what can and cannot be promised to the customer. In addition to directly improved revenue and sell-through, overcoming this business problem leads to an improved understanding of true demand. This is because most retailers are not capable of capturing data or intelligence on lost sales opportunities, only successful ones. The visibility solutions to this business problem depend on the retailer network and supply chain in question. There is not a one-size-fits-all approach. Bricks and mortar retailers tend to use one option, e-commerce uses another, and multichannel uses something else entirely.

Track and Trace of High Value Goods: Lot and Serial Number Tracking

Although current visibility technology includes solutions well beyond "track and trace" of imports, there are still demands for this type of service. Two special situations of increasing prominence in the "track and trace" arena are: tracking lot numbers and tracking serial numbers. The term "track and trace" is a generalization for technology and processes which allow decision makers to know the current location and lifecycle milestones of an item of interest while it is being transported. We already looked at a type of track and trace visibility at the start of this chapter, where retailers use track and trace to update plans based on the inbound supply chain. Track and trace type visibility is about products which are on the move, rather than inventory position or capacity planning, therefore track and trace visibility is more valuable for complex transport plans vs. simple transport plans. There is variation, but any good track and trace solution does the following:

1. Enables the user to track based on indirect attributes (order number, shipment number, item number, and so on).

2. Logs the actual, planned, and re-forecasted milestones for the item. The list should not be interrupted when the item moves from one physical shipment to another (such as via consolidation or deconsolidation).

3. Enables the item to be tracked by external parties over the web if they are granted permission. In other words, users do not have to be in a specific building, in a specific room, or on a special intranet in order to track and trace.

4. Enables some kind of alerting based on the item's status, such as email alert when the item arrives.

Most major logistics service providers offer track and trace visibility as a free or very inexpensive addition to their other services. Many of the logistics service providers use the same underlying technologies to do this: Log-Net, GT Nexus, Manhattan Associates, or INTRA. Other logistics service providers build in-house systems. UPS, for example, uses an in-house system called "Flex Global View." As a principle, tracking software will usually follow these guidelines:

1. Define the contents of a material handling unit.

2. Allow material handling units to be consolidated in to other material handling units, and later deconsolidated from them.

3. Record the location or status of the highest material handling unit.

4. Propagate the material handling unit status or location to its content material handling units and onward to their items.

What is meant by Material Handling Unit is any container, package, crate, truck, etc. which contains *other things*. For example, we could have 100 units of a DVD player in a box, and the box is considered a Material Handling Unit (or MHU). By tracking the location and status of the box, we simplify the tracking of its contents. Then, the box may be consolidated into a pallet with 30 other boxes. The pallet is now a new Material Handling Unit, and we track the pallet's location and status. If the pallet gets shipped to Shanghai, China, then we say all the contents of the pallet are also in Shanghai.

To give a more generic example, think about a human body. It's a safe assumption that one can track the body's physical location and then apply it to all of its limbs. The location of the hands and feet do not need to be defined separately from the head, neck, or torso. By grouping the limbs into a Material Handling Unit of "body," we simplify the process of tracking the person's various limbs. This mechanism is the basic building block behind tracking and tracing visibility, and also can be a headache when a Material Handling Unit is modeled incorrectly. For example, consider what happens when an ocean master bill of loading (MBOL) is considered the Material Handling Unit, but in fact it has two ocean containers and one is received into a destination warehouse on a Friday while the other waits until Monday. For several days the MBOL's status will be "delivered" or "pending deliver," and it will propagate down to all items it contains, and this means about half the items will have incorrect statuses. This example shows why the Material Handling Units have to be selected carefully during visibility solution design.

Track and trace type visibility has some special cases, such as tracking objects which change during their lifecycle (bulk grain, for example, which loses weight due to wind blowing off some grains from the top), or objects that have special features like lot numbers, pedigree, or serial numbers. Lot number tracking is focused on groups of items produced, inspected, packaged, or otherwise processed together. Lot number control is common in pharmaceuticals, agriculture products, foods, or engineering-intensive devices. A lot number may be assigned to a group of USB thumb-drives every time the machinery is re-calibrated. Or, a lot number may be assigned to a quantity of milk which is pasteurized in the same vat. In either situation, the assumption is that a defect, risk, or problem with *one item* from the lot raises the probability of the *other items* in the same lot having some similar issue.

Lot numbers are critical to safely recalling or stopping the flow of drugs or foods while not affecting every piece of that item's inventory. Beyond being costly, this may be a matter of life and death for some drugs, because discarding *all* of the products inventory would cause critical shortages. For a visibility process, tracking lot numbers is fairly straight forward. Every item is given an extra attribute called "Lot Number," and the lowest-level Material Handling Unit is usually forced to hold one and only one lot number. For example, a box which contains bottles of milk would be the lowest Material Handling Unit, and a business rule is established where the box can contain one, and only one, lot number. Of course, the box itself isn't part of the lot number. But, it speeds up the ability to isolate or destroy defective lots. An alternative is to have the lot number printed on the physical item (such as what happens with pharmaceuticals), and the Material Handling Unit has a data table with the lot number and related quantity information.

Unique serial number tracking is different from lot number tracking. Serial numbers are usually applied to *every* item, in an effort to control expensive items which need to be registered or serviced at a later date. For example, cars have serial numbers which enable people to ensure the identity of the car among thousands of other identical units. Serial number tracking is also used for gift cards or SIM cards, so that theft of the card can be mostly nullified via de-activating one, and only one, serial number without impacting the service of other legitimate customers.

As many practitioners have experienced, tracking lot numbers is very different from tracking serial numbers. Lot numbers are unique references which identify sets of items, often in discrete Material Handling Units. Serial numbers are an inversion of the lot number concept: a unique number which represents one, and only one, item as it co-mingles with potentially hundreds of thousands of other items. Because of this, and because of the way most track and trace type visibility systems are propagating data from higher Material Handling Units down to the items they hold, serial number tracking is a challenging process.

So, how to do serial number tracking type visibility successfully? The most important step is perfecting the data capture at both the supplier and the point of consumption. When a small box or bundle is first filled with 500 SIM cards and a barcode label is applied, that is the instant when the serial numbers (usually as a range) must be recorded against the barcode number. The barcode can then be treated in a similar way to a Material Handling Unit, where it can be aggregated with other boxes or bundles. If this crucial first step leaves data not captured, it is very expensive and error-prone to gather the data later. Even with a situation where a box or bundle breaks apart, and has to be re-boxed, the company may lose profit margin due to the high labor required to re-establish serial numbers to the new barcodes. Widespread adoption of RFID technologies may provide another, more flexible vector for capturing serial number data at later stages, or verifying data which was already captured. But most industries do not yet have ubiquitous RFID tagging and sensing.

If data is well captured at the initial point, the flowing of serial numbers through the supply chain channels can be tracked. This type of visibility almost always has a requirement that final consumption is also identified. For example, a mobile phone company might require visibility on every serial number, starting at production but ending with the contact details of the individual who bought the item and the employee ID of the sales staff who made the transaction. This could be used for fraud detection, warranty validation, or for after-sales support. The visibility application has to be ready to explode one box or bundle, which may have had 500 SIM cards and only required about 1,000 data points, into a miniature point of sales database. Even more challenging may be the last few days of a serial number's lifecycle. Once a box of SIM cards (same example again) arrives at a retailer, and the retail staff tear open the box, the serial numbers go into a kind of informational black-box. The visibility application knows the serial numbers were delivered, and also knows they were not sold yet. But, the visibility application usually doesn't have a positive-proof of location inside the retail store. Cycle counting or serial number rotation can be used, but they increase complexity and chances for manual error. In the future, RFID may be used to actively verify store inventory in situations like this, but it is not yet at sufficient adoption to be a useful design approach. For these reasons successful examples of end-to-end serial number tracking are usually reliant on a robust Point of Sales (POS) system to feed back the data on serial number consumption. Just as the visibility application needs near-perfect data about serial number packing from the manufacturer, it will need near-perfect serial number consumption data from the point of sale.

Track and tracing of lot and especially serial numbers is its own type of supply chain visibility. Although it is similar to the "world as a warehouse" model in the need for globally uniform visibility to materials, the two types of supply chain visibility differ in the need for a "closed loop" by connecting point of sales information back to the material's lifecycle. A good test to distinguish between those who need "world as a warehouse" type visibility and "serial or lot number track and trace" visibility is to ask if the supplier's and customer's details need to be connected with the material's historical data. For pharmaceuticals, spare parts on airplanes, laptops, and fresh food the answer is definitely "yes." The requirement to connect producer and consumer data to the material lifecycle, either back to production lot or to a single item via a serial number, is what makes this type of supply chain visibility unique.

Competitive Market Visibility

The historical assumption of supply chain visibility is that it is inward looking, meaning that the supply chain in question belongs to the organization that operates the visibility solution. By this default view, supply chain visibility is designed to improve self-awareness: to inventory, orders, capacity, and so forth. The other examples discussed in this chapter certainly support the historical view. But this doesn't always need to be the case, as discussed in the proposal of a new definition of supply chain visibility. In some situations, supply chain visibility is about seeing a *competitor's* supply chain and making competitive positioning decisions based on that understanding of how they bring their products to market. This is the "competitive market" type supply chain visibility.

One can imagine, given the difficulty supply chain managers have in knowing their own supply chain, how transparency to a competitor's supply chain would be difficult to achieve. The most challenging aspect of visibility to a competitor's supply chain is the data capture. Where a retailer may have trouble getting production plan data from their own suppliers, they have really no chance of getting such data interfaced to them from a competitor retailer's supplier (exempting illegal approaches of course). So, if supply chain managers can't simply ask for the data about their competitor, how do they get it? This is where things get interesting.

As a point of reference, constructing an understanding of the competitor's supply chain using legally available methods is something that often occurs during a hostile acquisition attempt. After all, the supply chain is a major determinate of a business's success, so it's therefore a determinate of the business's valuation and how well it would fit with the acquiring company's existing supply chain, IT systems, or management culture. In non-hostile acquisitions a lot of data is provided willingly by the target company, but this clearly wouldn't be the case when trying to setup supply chain visibility on a competitor. A lot of the processes done in evaluating hostile takeover targets are redeployed for competitive market type visibility. These processes include using publicly available data to estimate:

- Organization charts for sourcing, product development, IT, logistics, and sales.

- IT landscape, including what ERP is in place, what systems are used for forecasting, order management, inventory management, and so forth.

- Channels to market: do they have retail stores, do they have a web store, and so forth.

- Fixed assets in machinery or buildings. Knowing that a company owns its own distribution center may illuminate how they manage their supply chain.

- Timeline of major investments, entry into new markets, and so forth.

- Stated goals in new markets, with new products.

- Formal partnerships or sponsoring status of industry associations.

- Executive compensation schemes and backgrounds.

- Patents or ongoing legal disputes.

- Financial outlook: are they debt free, debt heavy, and so forth.

- Employee overview: how many, where at, and so forth.

- Ownership structure.

- Major suppliers and customers, with hopefully the same kind of analysis as described above being done on these supply chain partners.

For large public companies, virtually every point above can be discovered legally. In most cases, the data above form a kind of "master data" that allows the supply chain team to understand the macro-level forces affecting the competitor's supply chain. In some situations, keeping this updated in a CRM-type tool is enough. For example, its common practice for sales-staff to be required to keep ongoing notes about prospects or clients in a CRM tool. If the sales person sees someone at a conference and they mention that the vice-president of the prospect company has just been fired, the sales-person is supposed to go to the CRM tool and update it. This allows all sales staff, even in the future, to have a kind of collective memory about the client or prospect organization.

Just as the process of maintaining a collective memory about the prospect or client is very valuable, the same can be done with competitor supply chains. When the analysis shifts from the competitor as an individual company, to the competitor combined with their supply chain partners, we are talking about competitive market supply chain visibility. Perhaps more important is to take the "master data" types of information about the competitor supply chain and connect it with more transactional, real time data. The best data sources for transactional-level data on a competitor are government-mandated reporting. Governments are interesting as a data source. They are able to dictate the content, format, and quality of the data. Generally, the data they obtain becomes publicly available. In some situations, there is a delay, which renders the data less useful. And the public data may come in truly awful formats, such as a printed report which must then be re-keyed into a database to be useful. But, all of those issues aside, government data can be used to fill in transactional data on a competitor's supply chain.

Imagine, for example, a specialty manufacturer in the US selling industrial electrical fittings for public electric grid operators. Their competitor is also based in the US, since transporting the finished fittings is extremely expensive. Having done the analysis described earlier and keeping it maintained, they have a good overview of the competitor and their supply chain. Going into a request for quotations (RFQ), they leverage that visibility to improve the price quote decision. How would this be done? The answer lies with publicly available data from the government. In the USA, imports are recorded at a fairly transactional level and publicly available. With the right process or system, supply chain management can know the following about the competitor:

- Who are their suppliers?

- What exact materials or parts they have been buying?

- The quantity of materials or parts.

- The first price paid for the materials or parts.

- In what rhythm the transactions take place between the supplier and the competitor: daily, weekly, monthly, and so forth.

With the "master data" information collected periodically and transactional data about the exchanges between the competitor and their suppliers it should be possible to answer these questions:

- Does the competitor have materials on hand to handle this order, or would they issue a PO to their supplier (i.e. are we pricing against a make-to-stock or a make-to-order offer)?

- Given the expense of final-SKU transportation, what would be the expected transport cost from the competitor's facility vs. my own facility?

- Does the competitor use the same supplier, and if so:

  - Who buys more volume?
  - Who pays higher prices?
  - Who orders regularly vs. irregularly?
  - Is there an opportunity to lock-up capacity with the supplier by using the competitive market visibility information during negotiations?

These questions can help determine how the competitor will respond to the RFQ. Perhaps the competitor runs very lean and has no inventory of raw materials to fulfill an immediate order, but can sell for a lower price point if the order is delayed. Now the manufacturer knows where to compete, i.e. based on speed to deliver rather than price.

The transactional data a company has access to greatly depend on their industry and locality. Every country has its own government initiatives to collect data, and each industry has specific reporting requirements and data which are considered valuable. But in almost all situations there is some kind of supply chain transactional data leaking out which can be integrated into a competitive market supply chain visibility solution. For an excellent example of this kind of visibility in practice, take a look at the visibility solution from "Panjiva." This solution takes US government reporting on imports, does substantial data integration and cleansing, and then makes it available on a monthly subscription basis. In summary, this type of visibility is an inversion of the historical assumption that visibility is inward looking. Instead of trying to get more information on one's own inventory, or one's own order statuses, the competitive market type supply chain visibility tries to get this information about the direct competition.

Status Visibility

In general terms we can say that supply chain objects have a status; for example a "shipment" (object) is "in-transit" (status). Objects tend to be things like orders, order lines, shipments, Bills of Lading, containers, pallets, boxes, requisitions, claims, invoices, and so forth. In the "Status Visibility" type of supply chain visibility, the goal is to make all object statuses visible to decision makers. Often the status itself is less valuable for the decision maker than identifying status changes. In these situations, there may be more value in switching to an "event management" type of visibility. Below is an explanation of how these two types of visibility compare and why "status visibility" is more common as an approach.

Imagine a sourcing manager who has weekly touch bases with every supplier. Part of the meeting involves a review of the open Purchase Orders (POs), with special emphasis on any product which may not be in compliance with the contracted ship-dates on the PO. Prior to the meeting, the sourcing manager must have a report with the supplier's POs, the related shipments, the related work-in-progress updates, and finally the shipment schedules (including holidays) and connect all this data to forecast or identify PO late fulfillment. This is obviously time consuming and with a large number of suppliers may represent a full-time workload for a whole team of analysts.

Ideally, a supply chain visibility solution could be deployed here to automate most steps of the work. Gathering the data and connecting it is easy, and calculating the probability of lateness is also possible. The question would be, "how to store the result showing one PO is on time and another is late?" This is where the object status comes into play. Often times retail buyers want to work in the order management system and not have to conduct "swivel chair" integration by logging in and navigating through a visibility solution as well. By extending the possible statuses of the PO in the order management system to include feedback from the visibility system we enable the storage of the output in a format and system familiar to the sourcing manager. It's possible the sourcing manager never even sees the visibility application because it acts as a black-box, with the output integrated to the order management system. By looking for status changes in the order management system the sourcing manager can see which of her POs is at risk for being late simply by filtering the PO list on supplier and status code.

In some situations the company may want specific actions taken when a status changes. For example, when the status changes from "In-Transit" to "Damaged," an email notification might be sent out. Since statuses are enduring qualities, the solution can't tie the notification to the status itself. To give an example, the status "damaged" may stay in place for a week. Would the company want continuous emails because the status remains as "damaged"? Not likely. Instead, the company is looking for an alert when the status changes from one thing to another, which is basically a one-time event. This makes the supply chain visibility application a kind of Finite State Machine (FSM). The power of the FSM is that it can support many statuses, on many objects, as well as the special events which should occur during the cutover from one status to another. The compactness and utility of FSM is shown in the fact that most video games use them to model the Artificial Intelligence (AI) of the non-human players. If they can work in this context to react appropriately to almost limitless behaviors from the human player, they are capable of reacting to inputs from the supply chain data and updating supply chain objects accordingly. This isn't the place to go into the technical aspects behind finite state machines, but practitioners who are interested in implementing "status visibility" to an advanced level of maturity are encouraged to look into this further.

This description of "Status Visibility" probably sounds similar to "event management" type visibility. They do share a focus on knowing *when* something *happens* in the supply chain. But the two approaches are different in important ways. First, statuses endure and events do not. And conversely an event occurring on an object doesn't necessarily change the object's status. For some applications it's better to use statuses where the objects are being fundamentally changed as events occur. Second, statuses can only apply when an object exists. For example, what if 50 percent of a company's inbound supplies for the next week of manufacturing are going to be delivered late? An event approach can catch this, but a status visibility approach cannot because there is no object to which we can apply the status update. Certainly all the individual shipment, PO, or PO line objects could show a status of "late," but it would be up to the human users to connect the dots and realize that collectively the total lateness will be more than 50 percent of inbound supplies. Third, status visibility is particularly useful when the object and target statuses are already defined in external systems. For example, if a company has spent a lot of money, time, and energy rolling out an ERP system and that system tracks materials down to the individual case level, it makes sense to have the visibility system register events as status updates and pass that data to the ERP for further usage. Re-leveraging the object or status list from another application lowers the learning curve for getting a visibility solution in place and enables greater integration of the two system's capabilities. Finally, "Status Visibility" is probably an easier version of supply chain visibility to setup as compared to true event management. Event management should be able to support status updates as one of the possible actions automated when an event occurs. Event management can also use statuses as qualifying criteria for an event. For example an event might be called "Credit Risk" and it occurs when a PO with a supplier is in "late" status, and concurrently the supplier requests better credit terms or payment. Therefore many companies begin by thinking in terms of status visibility until they are dealing with events that are tied to multiple or no business object for which a status is tracked. At this point they may decide to graduate up to event management.

In summary, "status visibility" is a type of supply chain visibility which focuses on the current state of supply chain objects like POs, shipments, invoices, or material handling units. The best fit for this type of visibility is when the company has well defined objects, already manages those objects in other systems, and needs an automated "black box" to decide what state the object is in and to initiate actions as the state changes. As status visibility gets more complex, with many possible actions based on the starting and ending status during a status change, it looks more and more like event management type supply chain visibility. But the two types of visibility are indeed different. Events are instantaneous, whereas statuses endure. Also a status presupposes a business object, whereas events can be any logical pattern which evaluates to true or false. Finally, status visibility generally leverages the object definition and status list from other applications, so it is often an easier visibility type to implement compared to the more open-ended event management.

Conclusion of Visibility Types

The types of visibility listed in this chapter are those that many practitioners will, or have already, come across. They are the most popular formats at present and becoming familiar with them means one could follow most conversations about "supply chain visibility." This chapter is not exhaustive, of course. There are less common types of visibility, such as capacity visibility, which did not get discussed in this chapter but are still out there being used by real supply chains. As with most cataloging exercises, the hope is that by seeing a variety of what exists under the term "supply chain visibility" that the reader also identifies commonalities and how to deal with a new type when it emerges. The chapter closes now with a table comparing the visibility types which have been covered. The next chapter looks at the tools available to supply chain leaders who are ready to start their own supply chain visibility project.

Table 3.1   Summary of diverse visibility types

Supply Chain Visibility Type	Target Issue Addressed	Typical Industries
World as a Warehouse	What is the total view of all inventory, regardless of location?	· Consumer product brands · High Tech · Pharmaceutical · Heavy Manufacturing · FMCG
Lot and Serial Number Tracking	What happened during the lifecycle for a given product?	· High Tech · Pharmaceutical · Grocery and Food · Chemical · Spare parts and service · FMCG
GPS Tracking	What is the right physical location?	· Logistics Service Providers · Direct-to-Consumer · Driver Managed Inventory · Oil and Gas

Table 3.1   Continued

Supply Chain Visibility Type	Target Issue Addressed	Typical Industries
Inbound Track and Trace	Will inbound product arrive on time?	· Retail, especially in the USA · Heavy manufacturing · Oil and Gas
Save the Sale	Can the customer be promised something?	· Retail · E-commerce retailers
Competitive Market	What is happening in my competitor's supply chain?	· Consumer product brands · High Tech
Event Management	Given a pattern of facts which I think is important, what actions should be taken?	· Consumer product brands · High Tech · Pharmaceutical · Retail · FMCG
Status Visibility	Given all the supply chain's activity, is a given object in its expected status?	· Consumer product brands · Retail

4

Options for Acquiring Visibility Technology

This chapter examines the acquisition options for visibility technology, specifically from the point of view of a supply chain manager who is interested in improving or installing a supply chain visibility solution. The "market" in this chapter refers to services, software, or hardware that are available to supply chain managers.

An Overview of the Technology Market for Supply Chain Visibility

The enablement of supply chain visibility typically comes down to technology. Other inputs, like process engineering and human resources, are very important as well. Organizational factors such as organizational willingness were also discussed in Chapters 1 and 2. But selecting skilled staff or training those staff is beyond the scope of this book. The deeper reason to spend more time on the acquisition of visibility technology is in response to the prevailing view among practitioners that this is a critical area for visibility and also an area poorly covered by the current supply chain visibility literature. It is one of the topics of most concern among supply chain leaders when it comes time to design a new visibility solution or improve an existing solution. For supply chain visibility technology acquisition, there are effectively four approaches available:

1.   Build the technology in-house or through contracted development firms.

2.   Buy "complete off the shelf" (COTS) technology as an asset from another party (such as licensed software).

3.   Rent technology on a service arrangement, where a technology company provides not just the licensed software but also the active

method for deploying it. The asset remains with the supplier, and the cost is treated as an operating expense rather than an asset purchase for the buyer.

4.   Borrow the technology by using a company to provide a related service, and then leverage their technology at little or no costs.

None of the four approaches described above is dominant in all dimensions of interest. The practitioner interview transcripts in Appendix A show divergent views on which of these formats for acquiring visibility is best.

In-house development is surely the preferred approach if the technology will be one of the principle competitive aspects of the company. For example, Wal-Mart invested heavily in the late 1980s and early 1990s in inventory planning and visibility systems. Their ability to better manage inventory lifecycles was one of their core competitive dimensions, and so it would make no sense for Wal-Mart to have used technology available in the market because their competitors could easily adopt it if Wal-Mart proved successful. At the same time, the level of investment needed to achieve truly differentiating technology may be substantial. In the example of Wal-Mart, their investment in their proprietary "Retail Link" required deploying the world's largest private satellite network in 1988 (Småros, 2005).

Licensed software is typically faster to deploy than in-house development, benefits from a larger group providing feedback for improvements, and enables the company to find well skilled staff in the market place and therefore avoid some expertise-shortages. Off the shelf software makes sense when the company should have total control of the technology once it is deployed, but does not want to "redesign the wheel." An airline, for example, is totally dependent on its asset management capabilities. It would be dangerous (in a business sense) to allow the technology for managing airline assets to be dependent on external companies, which is why core systems are usually developed in-house or purchased off the shelf. But, since airline asset management is complex and also mature, it's unlikely that it is best suited to in-house development. As a rule of thumb, maturity of business requirements leads to less likelihood that an in-house developed solution will have break-away levels of competitive differentiation or performance improvement. In short, it's not advised to build in-house if the system is a mature commodity in the market.

Software (or any other visibility technology) is often available as a "rented" service. A generic term for this approach is "Software as a Service," although often times the service includes not just the software but the computational hardware to run it. The more marketing savvy providers also call this "cloud computing," a vague term which conflates software as a service with the tenancy mix (i.e. is one or multiple companies sharing the logical or physical system). This is sometimes called "paying by the drink," as opposed to "paying by the bottle" (purchasing software as an asset). At the heart of the service approach is the idea that a company may not want to purchase a technology outright and hold it as an asset. They may, instead, choose to contract a company to allow them to use the technology. The costs are then treated as operating expenses, and there should be a lower upfront cost. The tradeoff for lower up-front costs is a possible higher long-term cost as the incremental charges accumulate. In the year 2013 there is a considerable migration occurring among thought leaders about how much of an organization can or should be placed into cloud or SaaS arrangements. Just as the 1990s had a wave of thought leaders who suggested that organizations should outsource and insource and generally only hold on to those operations which are core differentiators, there seems to be a shift towards only holding technologies which are core differentiators and acquiring the others as services. But this view is not uniform: many leading supply chains will not entertain options for critical systems to be "in the cloud," either for security or control reasons.

Analysts already agree that software as a service makes sense for secondary or tertiary activities, where the loss of the service provider will not have serious, company-wide implications. Secondary or tertiary activities also make sense because these are aspects of a business which are last to be considered for large-sum up-front investment. Payroll processing, for example, is a secondary aspect of most companies. While it must be done (and done correctly), there is no competitive benefit in investing money in payroll processing. For a retailer, for example, the decision to open a new store or invest in a payroll processing technology is quite obviously going to result in a new store investment simply because the store offers a chance to grow the business whereas payroll processing does not.

Finally, in some situations a company will offer its business partners the option to use its visibility system as a perk of continuing to do business. This can be thought of as borrowing visibility technology. Sourcing agencies like Li & Fung offer visibility and order management systems as a perk for using them in the middle-man role of sourcing agent. Logistics service companies, like DHL, provide free or almost-free technology usage rights for visibility on anything they are paid to move. The e-commerce retailer Amazon offers inventory management software for small-scale retailers in exchange for listing

Table 4.1   Matrix of supply chain technology approach and business fit

	Private Development	Off the Shelf Technology	Technology as a Service	Technology as a Perk
High Criticality of Business Needs	Good	Good	Poor	Poor
Likely Competitive Differentiator	Good	Poor	Poor	Poor
Business Needs are Mature for the Industry	Poor	Good	Good	Good
Minimal initial investment	Poor	Poor	Good	Good
Minimal long term costs	Poor	Good	Poor	Good

that inventory on their web-store. The white-goods leader Haier provides point of sale systems to small retailers in 3rd tier cities in China, as long as they sell only Haier product lines and not the competitors' as well. The service provider's strategy here is quite clear: offer a supply chain visibility technology which competes well with an otherwise expensive in-house development or technology purchase and in doing so it makes the engagement more "sticky." The business partner (mostly customers, but sometimes suppliers) is agreeing to a trade-off, usually with the intention to make it temporary. From the customer's view, this option results in the least ability to control or customize the technology. Building in-house, buying off the shelf, or even renting technology from a specialist all offer more control of the functional scope. But this is the lowest cost option, in terms of up-front costs, ongoing costs, and even staffing costs. The cost-to-quality tradeoff will be most appealing for aspects which are not mission-critical, not competitively differentiating, and for small-to-medium sized companies, especially if they are growing quickly and therefore cash-starved.

Innovation Dictates Planning Horizon

The next chapter will proceed with a review of the major technology options from vendors (buy or rent), the following chapter addresses technology components (build in-house), and then there is a chapter on acquiring visibility as a service provided by a logistics company to improve their overall value-add (borrowing visibility). But across all four methods for acquiring supply chain visibility technology one should bear in mind that *the pace of innovation is the most important factor for the planning horizon* of the buy-rent-build-borrow decision. Technology is changing fast, and the rate of change is itself increasing. This rate of change needs to be considered in at least these ways:

- The reviews and advice given in the book will age quickly. Every vendor in the market will be releasing new versions of their software or services between the time when this chapter is written and when it is being read. This sentiment was also expressed in analyst reviews of the software options in the market (Cap Gemini, 2012).

- Just as the book's views have a short period of applicability, so do the views of any other industry participant such as consultants or a reader's colleagues. Don't assume that the best vendor two years ago is still the best, or that a colleague's bad experience with a provider is enough to disqualify them. This space is dynamic.

- Don't base any planning horizons on a five-year or greater period. Too much will change in the underlying business needs for visibility. As an example, five years ago the iPhone had not been released. Today, the need for visibility systems to work well with mobile computing (including smartphones like the iPhone and Android devices) is considered one of the premier pressure points for vendors. In short, if a company needs more than five years to earn the appropriate return or to get the technology rolled-out, it indicates the project will likely fail to deliver relevant visibility processes in the business context of the unknowable future.

- Pay attention to the scalability of the technology, especially as regards to data. Nearly every advance in technology related to supply chain visibility will increase data volume. Be prepared for this in the planning horizons. Systems that do well at one data volume may become a nightmare at higher data volumes.

- The selection of a new technology is also the selection of a future legacy system: no matter how well chosen, at some point within 10 years it is likely that the technology will be replaced or upgraded. One should plan for both onboarding and end of life migration when selecting the technology.

- People always underestimate the extent to which new innovations are available, or to the extent they will be impactful. In other words, there is a tendency to feel as though the present is a culmination of previous technology trends rather than a mid-point on the way to later ones. Try to plan as though new technological options and expectations will become available very often. With that assumption, the emphasis on adaptability and agility will grow and one will spend less time trying to "think through" the topic perfectly up-front and accept that new facets or business needs will emerge and cannot be forecasted based on the present state of business.

At the end of this book, there is also some space dedicated to discussing the most important changes in technology which may be factors to consider when making a visibility technology acquisition decision.

5

Buy or Rent: Software Vendors for Supply Chain Visibility

While writing this book it was hard to find a good way to review the available software vendor options. There are many software vendors, and in most cases they each release multiple software versions per year. Given the pace of technology change, within 18 months a direct review of their latest software would be outdated. There is also an issue with balanced exposure, because the author has deep experience with some software and very little with others. Speaking from personal experience would provide unbalanced coverage of the software providers. Also, not all vendors wanted their software reviewed in a side-by-side fashion. The next section tries to balance the risks these issues pose, with the hope of providing the reader with a good introduction to the supply chain visibility vendors.

Buyers of supply chain visibility software are at a significant disadvantage in the marketplace. Unlike ERP, order management, CRM, Business Intelligence, or other mature enterprise software markets there is little or no analyst coverage. Technology analyst organizations like Forrester and Gartner are not actively publishing about supply chain visibility as a class of software. It is unlikely to see side-by-side comparisons of the software vendors, hardware vendors, or service offering. One notable exception is a study conducted in 2012 by Cap Gemini which reviewed a fairly large set of supply chain visibility technology vendors (Cap Gemini, 2012). Interested readers can use the link in the referenced works section to obtain a copy of the study, contact Cap Gemini to get more details, or to see if a more recent version has been released.

The software market for supply chain visibility solutions shows medium-maturity in terms of market share consolidation. By one estimate, 75 percent of visibility solutions come from 25 percent of the market vendors (Cap Gemini, 2012). There are three or four major vendors in the supply chain visibility software market, but also dozens of smaller vendors competing on niche or price. In any given region or for a given type of visibility the smaller vendors may actually have stronger products or match the major vendors in functionality while leading them on price. Most of the vendors will also act as an outsourced software house and produce deep modifications or totally bespoke software for their clients if requested. In summary, the market for supply chain visibility technology is:

- Opaque, because few independent analysts are providing regular coverage, vendor comparisons, and so forth.

- Fractional, because so many software vendors and software versions exist.

- Highly niche, because regional and functional specialization is common.

Supply Chain Visibility Patents

The practice of patenting software, or software meta-designs, is controversial. The software development community has not achieved consensus in the idea that software should be patent-protected (as opposed to copyright protected, which is less controversial). Among the major markets for creation and sale of visibility technology, only the USA and Japan allow for software patenting. The EU, including the UK, specifically prohibits software as a category of patentable inventions. Often, the patenting process in the USA is simply done to have the capacity to lock up a competitor in costly legal battles. Some components of supply chain visibility technology, both software and hardware, have been patented in the USA and a review of those patent holders can help give an indication of who is most active in the applied R&D of this space. Table 5.1 opposite shows US patent holders for supply chain visibility inventions, by year of patent filing.

Several points are worth addressing regarding the patent holding patterns from the table above. First, there is considerable patent-seeking from military-sector participants. This contrasts with findings by Cap Gemini in 2012 that most supply chain visibility technology vendors are not active in aerospace or defense industries (Cap Gemini, 2012). Savi Technologies was an early developer of active RFID technologies for asset tracking, and were acquired by Lockheed Martin in 2006. In late 2012 they were sold to a private equity

Table 5.1   Supply chain visibility United States' patents by filing year

Company	Prior to 2000	2000 to 2005	2006 to 2010	2011 and 2012	Total Patents
UPS	1	5	4		10
Savi Technologies		7	1		8
Individual Inventors		2	3	1	6
E2Open		4	1		5
SAP		3	2		5
Accenture	1	2		2	5
Boeing	1		3		4
Visible Assets Inc			4		4
Oracle		3			3
Navitag Technologies		2			2
US Department of Energy				2	2
eSilicon		2			2
iSupply		2			2
Microsoft		1			1
Inner Circle Logistics		1			1
Entercoms				1	1
Checkpoint Systems			1		1
Afilias			1		1
Cisco		1			1
i2			1		1
Google			1		1
Rush Tracking System			1		1
Motorola		1			1
Manugistics		1			1

firm, but during their most active period they were focused on the military sector. Likewise, Boeing is active in the military sector. The second point is that the most active patent-seeking companies in this space are those who leverage a mix of proprietary hardware and software. The major vendors selling only software are not really dominant in this list.

Background on the Software Vendors

The three most important supply chain visibility software vendors are probably Log-Net, GT Nexus, and Manhattan Associates. A potential fourth would be E2Open, based on their patent-seeking activity and size. The claim that these are the most important vendors can't be quantified because there are no consistent published statistics on aspects such as the number of active customers, R&D investment, and the breadth of functionality. GT Nexus and Log-Net are pure visibility providers and are taken as established benchmarks against which new vendors often measure themselves. Manhattan Associates sells a broad and interconnected suite of supply chain management software (anchored to their flagship products of warehouse management systems) and is widely considered the premier software vendor for the supply chain domain. These three vendors offer widely different approaches to visibility, and none appears to dominate the others outright.

Second tier vendors of interest are either niche players who truly are differentiated, such as Panjiva, or extensions to supply chain software suites or ERP systems, including Oracle, SAP, Red Prairie, and JDA. These vendors usually do not compete head-to-head with the three main vendors described above. Instead, they target prospective customers who either have very specific needs or those who are already customers of another product and where the synergy of relationship or technology will give them an advantage.

Finally there are many third-tier supply chain visibility software vendors. These vendors are either extremely niche or are so small they focus on only one industry or geography. Super-niche providers include Descartes' eCellerate software which is purchased by many logistics service providers (especially freight forwarders) for its global trade management features. As an example, the second largest global freight forwarder Kuehne & Nagel purchased this system but simply plug it in as a feature of their larger visibility solution which is developed in-house. An example of the third-tier vendors who are not niche but just smaller players in the market is Amber Roads, formerly called Management Dynamics. In the future they may grow to become a significant supply chain visibility software vendor, but for now they are not active in the larger deals. Here is a table indicating approximate importance of the vendors in this space.

Table 5.2   Supply chain visibility technology vendors by importance

Most Important	Important	Niche
GT Nexus and TradeCard	Oracle	IBM's Sterling Commerce
Log-Net	Amber Road	Panjiva
Manhattan Associates	JDA/Red Prairie	Descartes eCellerate
E2Open		SAP

In the next part of this chapter three major supply chain visibility vendors are reviewed in more detail.

Manhattan Associates

Manhattan Associates, headquartered in Atlanta, Georgia, is a vendor of supply chain management solutions. Manhattan Associates is rooted in supply chain software via its warehouse management systems, which they brought to market starting over 20 years ago. The company is public, expanding, in good financial health, and has offices around the world. Several years ago, they made a strategic decision to converge their individual software solutions into a single business process platform called SCOPE. This aligned technical architecture, workflows, human factor design, and pretty much everything else about the software. This convergence to SCOPE is not complete for all the software they provide, but enough major systems have been consolidated and then deployed that the approach has proved itself. Each step towards a fully consolidated offering makes them stronger, including in the supply chain visibility space. They have already moved their supply chain visibility product to SCOPE and seen the related benefits for customers who leverage it. As explained by a director of product strategy for Manhattan Associates during an interview:

> Our approach is to separate the concept of supply chain visibility from the software solution, essentially creating a critical piece of technology infrastructure that provides visibility as a service to the rest of the enterprise. We have various software solutions which rely on visibility and also provide feeds in to it. So we separate visibility and event management from the core solutions. We suggest that the inability to separate these would be limiting, because no single operating aspects will provide visibility itself. In our approach, the platform delivers visibility as a side aspect of the main solutions. We do have the autonomy to offer a supply chain visibility software solution by itself, but we have found that the majority of successful visibility projects stem from a larger supply chain execution challenge. For example, that visibility is critically tied to DC execution, demand management, transport management, and so forth. This might be because it's hard to put an ROI on visibility. For years, CIOs rank visibility as an area of interest but tend to get cut from the list of funded projects because it is challenging to identify the ROI for a standalone visibility project. In today's world of the empowered customer, the need for visibility is a

critical step to bring your supply chain closer to your end customer and therefore create the unwavering loyalty every business wants (Fenwick, Appendix A).

For supply chain visibility Manhattan Associates leverages several software packages, but they do have a standalone product called "Extended Enterprise Management" or "EEM" for short. The EEM application is available in two flavors: a Microsoft-architecture version and an open-systems or IBM architecture version. The open systems version is the newer one, is integrated into SCOPE, and should be the default system selected unless a prospective buyer is only able to work with Microsoft servers.

STRENGTHS

- Manhattan Associates' EEM is a credible, proven technology with good references behind it.

- The USA disaster response organization "FEMA" uses EEM for emergency logistics visibility and many Forbes 40 retailers also use it, indicating the EEM software has wide flexibility for purpose.

- Manhattan Associates has active offices in more places than their competitors, and has deployed to clients in broader geographic and industry ranges.

- The application is the leader in the "world as a warehouse" model, and has proven deployments for managing case-level unique identifiers (i.e. LPNs).

- Manhattan Associates are conservative and careful about their sales cycle. It's unlikely (but not impossible) they will over commit on functionality.

WEAKNESSES

- Manhattan Associates best centers of professional staffing for supply chain visibility are in Europe and the USA. If a buyer is not in these regions, they must be sure to be clear about which professional service consultants will be on their project, their experience, and if they must cover travel costs.

- The EEM software is licensed, which translates into higher up-front costs for the software and also the hardware, but lowers the long-term costs. This can make a one to two year comparison look favorable for the SaaS providers.

- As a software, EEM is much more attractive when combined with other SCOPE software, like the distributed order management or the warehouse management solutions.

- The EEM software can be difficult to deploy. As a licensed software, the buyer must be ready to administer not just the software but the users and the interface feeds between supply chain parties.

- The conversion to a technical platform is largely complete, but at some point that platform will probably need to be converted again to enable a SaaS delivery model. This will take time and resources, and slow new feature additions compared to competitors who began as SaaS solutions.

GT Nexus

GT Nexus is a private company started in 1999, based in California but with offices in several other markets. They have grown very rapidly and now pose a serious challenge to established vendors like Manhattan Associates, and have largely bypassed Log-Net. GT Nexus bases its business model on a multi-tenet hosted solution, where all parties connect into one instance that acts as a "community" portal for supply chain activities. This gives new members of the community instant benefits because all the required connections are likely to be covered in existing "pipes" from major industry players, like steamship lines. The downside is the need to constantly comply with community needs, rather than doing what is best for an individual client. GT Nexus offers some light planning or optimization tools for shippers or LSPs, but these are weak in comparison to true TMS solutions. In late 2012 they merged with TradeCard, another supply chain SaaS provider whose offering was complimentary to the GT Nexus functional scope. TradeCard focuses on the financial control, planning, and execution as regards international supply chains. It is too early to tell what the merger will achieve, but both companies have done very well and grown quickly on their own. Their combined employee count will be over 1,000 and this puts them in to the same league as major supply chain software players like JDA, Red Prairie, and Manhattan Associates. If they can behave synergistically they are likely to become the dominant vendor in this space. Probably more telling, both TradeCard and GT Nexus have already mastered the art of multitenant SaaS deployment, and this puts them at a tremendous head start to their competitors.

STRENGTHS

- Constantly perfecting their sales approach, GT Nexus is growing quickly and that growth benefits their entire customer base because of the "community" factor of a multi-tenant SaaS product. Their industry penetration in retail, fashion, and hi-tech manufacturing are extensive. They are well connected to ocean steam ship lines, and some 3PLs like CEVA or DB Schenker.

- They have established a large community now, which gives them a realistic advantage when dealing with a big customer rollout and also shows they understand data management. Their master data model is best among the major vendors.

- They have frequent version releases, which allow them to bring new functionality to market quickly.

- As a SaaS model, they can under-cut the start-up costs of licensed software vendors like Manhattan Associates.

WEAKNESSES

- GT Nexus has effectively one software and all their clients are users. They cannot make rapid changes or revisions to that software's fundamentals because of the effect it would have on the client base. This makes them less agile for *deep* functionality changes, even if it makes them more agile for minor changes.

- GT Nexus is still broadly used in only two key import markets, the US and the EU.

- GT Nexus has a reputation of over-selling and it's possible to find ex-clients or current clients who complain about this.

- The GT Nexus functionality is order-centric, and if the data model needs to have another base (such as inventory, capacity plans, or forecasts) this is going to be an issue.

- Over longer time periods they are relatively expensive compared to Log-Net (also a SaaS provider) and will be much more expensive for large companies when compared to licensed or developed software. But for SMEs with low transaction counts they may be less expensive than licensed or developed software, regardless of the time horizon.

Log-Net

Log-Net is a privately owned company founded in 1991 in New Jersey, USA. They have offices in Seattle and Hong Kong. The company was primarily focused on visibility systems for logistics service providers (LSPs), then later with global trade compliance, and most recently have added order and transportation optimization functions. They offer single tenant hosted solutions. Log-Net has a wide install base among LSPs and some retailers such as Home Depot.

STRENGTHS

- Functionally, arguably the strongest supply chain visibility suite available in the market. They are notably ahead in several areas.

- Log-Net is an engineering-oriented company. From a functional perspective, their service provides a good function-per-investment ratio.

- Log-Net's development priorities appear to be set by the CEO and founder. The advantage is that he has often selected priorities correctly, even when they might not have satisfied immediate client demands.

- The founders are still with the company and they are fiscally conservative, with a long-term orientation.

- Log-Net has served some of the most stringent client security requirements while maintaining a SaaS approach. For example they can host instances on shared or independent hardware, and so forth. This is a critical differentiator from GTNexus, who hosts all clients into a single instance (i.e. they leverage multitenant cloud).

WEAKNESSES

- They have a reputation of a poor ability to sell, particularly if the decision hinges on non-functional considerations. The buying team reviewing their proposal may be less engaged by their sales style.

- Log-Net has a reputation of being conservative in their targets and commitments to prospects or clients, which makes them appear to be less innovative even though their R&D achievements are as good as the competitors.

- Relatively small company for the scope of product they want to sell.

- Geographically focused in the US, with limited engagements elsewhere.

Comparing the Major Vendors

No vendor is dominant in all categories. For pure supply chain visibility Log-Net appears the strongest provider, although they have no coverage of world as a warehouse or serial and lot number tracking types of visibility. Both of those types of supply chain visibility are best handled by Manhattan Associates. For all but the largest organizations, GT Nexus may be the best option if large portions of their trading partners are already active in the GT Nexus platform. Because GT Nexus is the only serious multi-tenant solution, it has a tremendous advantage when the deployment community overlaps with its existing user base.

The differences in functionality between the three major vendors are important, but in many areas they are not as differentiating as the business models being used. For example, a retailer trying to answer business questions like "can I promise to distribute inventory that is in-transit" will have about the same level of overall support from all three vendors' software. But the business model and therefore delivery method for supporting the retailer will be different. Therefore potential visibility software buyers need to make a conscious decision regarding which model they are most aligned to, i.e. multi-tenet SaaS, single-tenet SaaS, or licensed software. It will dictate their ability to differentiate, the resources they need in house, and their end-of-life plan to a great extent.

In exercises where the three software options are evaluated with the supply chain visibility scorecard, they tend to have similar but overall low fitness scores. This seems to indicate the relative immaturity of the software available. All three software options focus on gathering data and making it accessible, which shows in the scorecards having higher scores in the first two metrics. Accessible data is good, but doesn't directly generate value. A fully mature software offering would complete the cycle by identifying what parts of that data were relevant, crunch it into information, and then interrupt the decision-making process in a beneficial way. Manhattan Associates has some case studies where this kind of full decision support is occurring. But these clients are achieving full decision support by using multiple Manhattan Associates solutions, such as supply chain visibility plus a distributed order management application to execute automatic inventory allocation decisions. It's a powerful combination of software, but more expensive because of the breadth of functionality involved. If a prospective visibility software buyer would be interested in a larger suite from Manhattan Associates, this is a serious option to consider.

In summary, none of these three main software providers has killer, irreplicable, proprietary tools in their offering. This isn't to say they are undifferentiated: Log-Net offers a well-balanced functional suite, especially attractive on a cost-per-transaction basis. Manhattan Associates clearly provides the best "world as a warehouse" type of visibility and has a hard-to-reproduce integration with its other (market leading) supply chain software. GT Nexus has superb master data management and a pre-built network of companies already on-board, which is especially strong in the apparel and retail sectors. The GT Nexus "community" can be a huge, decision-turning factor for SMEs who would otherwise have to bootstrap their own network. GT Nexus's model may even one day become the de-facto portal for supply chain visibility, most likely in some key industries like retail.

Vendor Trends and Maturity

The biggest changes in the supply chain visibility software space in 2012 and 2013 have been on mobile computing, the rise in SaaS solutions, and user interface improvements (human factors engineering). All these trends tie into larger technology streams, such as the explosion of smartphone and tablet computer form factors. The interest in SaaS solutions was noted by almost every practitioner interview (Appendix A), by analyst reports (Aberdeen

Group, 2012; Cap Gemini, 2012), and in the messaging coming from the vendors themselves. Most of these comments showed not just interest in the trend but a strong prediction that SaaS is the more appropriate approach for most visibility needs (Cap Gemini, 2012; interviews in Appendix A). It is likely that on-premise license and install software will not be the predominate ownership model for supply chain visibility in the near future.

As regards to mobile computing, between 2009 and 2013 the density of workers with mobile devices, and also the capabilities of those devices, has exploded. It's now reasonable to assume that a high proportion of the users interacting with a supply chain visibility solution have a high performing computing device with them at all times. This shift has come largely without clear strategies or ideas about why this is better for the business. It's interesting that we can track order statuses from our iPhones while on the toilet, but there is a dearth of well-articulated ideas about how and why doing so will improve business performance. Many studies suggest that the opposite is true: that the best employees are diluted and their effectiveness is diminished when they switch to working longer hours at low intensity.

The three major supply chain visibility software vendors have approached visibility and mobility quite differently. GT Nexus and Log-Net have developed iPad and iPhone versions of their user interface. Their target persona seems to be a manager in a developed market, probably working for a company which does importing and uses the supply chain visibility software to get an update on some key order or shipment, even perhaps to view a periodic report. The iPhone and iPad format is not effective for intense or prolonged usage: a core user who spends hours with the software every day would simply want a keyboard and mouse.

Manhattan Associates has focused on a completely different aspect of mobility: the operations in material handling sites like hubs, pickup drivers visiting a store, or store staff receiving stock into their backroom. These users need reliable, asynchronous, industrial-grade mobile devices. The application doesn't look graphically rich and pretty, but simple and can be used without training. This targeted mobility functionality is well aligned with their core strengths in the "world as a warehouse" visibility model. It's also much more defensible as a business function because there are real labor savings when the worker is made mobile compared to being tethered to a stationary computer and constant internet access. For example, if a retailer takes delivery at a mall the store staff may have to sign for their delivery and let the driver leave before all the stock is in the backroom. If they can only scan to verify the cartons in the backroom, they lose a key opportunity to quality control the delivery with the driver present. With a mobile device running asynchronously the store staff can do this at the delivery dock without the need for a live and fast internet connection. In the mobile computing area, Manhattan Associates has a stronger strategy and offering, even if it is less pretty in sales presentations.

User Interface and Supply Chain Visibility

The usability of a software's human interface is important inversely proportional to user count. That sounds a bit complicated but it will make sense with a few examples. First, consider modern jet fighter planes. Their human interface and controls are extremely complicated. But that is not a problem because the user community (fighter pilots) is extensively trained for using the interface. In effect, the human is modified to meet the system. Now consider an iPhone: with hundreds of millions of users even 30 minutes of training represents an incredible burden to the provider. For a mass-deployed technology the human interface must be as close as possible to self-training, via an interested user experience offering low-risk explore and learn options. The graphic above depicts how the investment in design is balanced with the investment in user training. The supply chain visibility system is cost-optimal when the left and right side of the equation are made equal, which occurs by tweaking factors A and B. But, like the iPhone example above, the size and diversity of the group is also critical. In short, the user base for supply chain visibility software has been growing and diversifying in terms of usage goals, educational background, and geographic location. Software providers of supply chain visibility are responding by delivering more usable systems, but their efforts and successes have not been equal.

The winner in terms of improved user interface would probably be Log-Net. Again, this can't be quantitative because there is no public publishing of

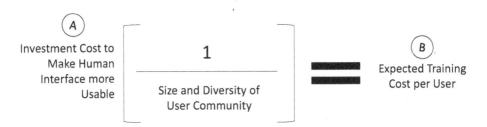

Figure 5.1   Balancing usability vs. training costs

usability metrics and the vendors are not facilitating side by side comparisons on this topic. Log-Net has adopted a rather forward thinking approach on several user-interface related topics. The first user interface topic where they excel is in the setup and sharing of interface customizations. They have a "dashboard push" technology which allows users to offer their user interface customizations to each other. To get specific on this, consider an example of several hundred users where each one has a personal unique UI layout. If a new layout is tested by one user, and proves to be useful, they can broadcast this as an optional dashboard layout for others to try and use. Succeeding with the functionality here is a delicate balance; the other software providers have similar but slightly less impactful variants. GT Nexus allows administrators to make an update in user layouts, but this must be done:

1. As an administrator.

2. Is final rather than made as an option which the user can try themselves.

3. Must be done on a user group basis.

Similarly, Manhattan Associates has the ability to change all users within a specific role group, so they adopt a new layout. But the limitations are:

1. Only one layout is available per user.

2. The layout is assigned by administrators only.

3. It must be done on a user group basis.

Log-Net's approach appears to be functionally superior for the user and represents a lower cost of ownership for the company.

The second area where Log-Net differentiates its user interface is in their customizability. Each user can customize their UI with a high degree of flexibility. This is done via a kind of "re-skinning" of the UI to address style-sheet level issues. Font, color, and style are all in scope. This is well beyond the options even an administrator could use in GT Nexus or Manhattan Associates' product offering. And, again, we're talking about options available to the end-user directly without admin or super-user mediation. With Log-Net the clear winner in customization, who would come second? It's really a tie, because the user-specific customization in GT Nexus and Manhattan Associates' products are quite similar. Manhattan Associates has greater options for custom labeling of the screen, including double-byte enabled languages, whereas GT Nexus offers a better user experience with things like column arrangement and saved sorting defaults.

The last specific user interface difference which deserves note is that Log-Net has a more functional dashboard landing page. Dashboard utility can be measured by the proportion of active user time that takes place from the dashboard as opposed to all other pages in the application. It could also be measured in terms of click-path depth, where the effective dashboard has a higher ratio of click-path roots which begin in the dashboard, indicating a user starts with something in the dashboard and then drills-in to deal with specific situations. Log-Net is targeting the dashboard as a "to-do list" and offers one very unique support for that need: the Log-Net dashboard is constantly refreshing while allowing the user to work in parallel portlets. Here is an example: imagine a user is required to approve certain air freight plans prior to departure, and the dashboard is designed to show the list of pending air freight shipments as well as total transport spend for the week. In GT Nexus or Manhattan Associates' products the user would need to deal with these two items separately, which is challenging because they may make the approval decision in light of total transport spend for the week. In Log-Net the dashboard could show both factors (and without an admin having to set it up), and when the user clicks to approve an air freight shipment in one part of the screen the other part is refreshed in real time. This is a break-away improvement in the functional power of the dashboard when compared to the other major vendors.

Overall Market Maturity for Supply Chain Visibility Software

The supply chain visibility market is consolidating. It is past the early shake-out phase where dozens or hundreds of potentially viable software was on offer, but not yet at the phase where technology lock-in is stabilizing to two or three larger players as the de-facto market owners. There are many software options for supply chain visibility, but only three or four are truly available globally and deployed among many companies. Log-Net, GT Nexus, and Manhattan Associates are continuing to take customers from each other in an apparently random churn. But in terms of total growth, GT Nexus appears to be bringing more clients on board to its visibility solution that its direct competitors. However, none of the vendors has pulled ahead or made such deep integration

within the customer's landscape that they are unable or unwilling to cut out
the software for short-term gains. Anecdotally, it may have been reasonable
to build a custom database management system 15 years ago, but today they
have reached technical capabilities that are just not cost effective to build from
scratch. The same applies to ERP systems, which no one in their right mind
would build from scratch today. But what about supply chain visibility? In
this space it's still possible that a custom application can meet or exceed off the
shelf solutions for many companies or use cases, and do so at a lower total cost
of ownership. As Cap Gemini stated in their report on the state of the supply
chain visibility software market in 2012:

> *The number of implementations is a relevant indicator for the size of
> the market, however, no real market leader can be identified. Five of the
> 20 selected vendors are responsible for 73 percent of the total number
> of implementations over the last three years. However, the complexity
> and size of the implementations itself is not considered. In terms of
> turnover there are several large players, but these players often have
> revenues from other business/supply chain management solutions and
> services. Since one or two market leaders still need to develop dominant
> positions, this gives room for smaller companies and start-ups to gain
> or enter the market for visibility solutions (Cap Gemini, 2012).*

Ultimately, what is disappointing in the pace and direction of the software
development for supply chain visibility is the lack of fully integrating the
components into something truly exceeding what can be done with just more
people. Market participants, particularly consultants and software vendors,
often comment that supply chain visibility is less interesting in low labor-cost
countries. In those markets it is a constant struggle for software vendors to
explain why the same visibility benefits couldn't be achieved by just throwing
more staff with Excel spreadsheets at the problem. With today's software
the "more people" solution is not so crazy. In part, this is because supply
chain visibility is a process which could always be done manually at some
cost and speed. Here is an analogy: Charles Babbage realized that one could
split advanced calculations down to simple arithmetic and have dozens or
hundreds of lower-educated workers execute them in parallel. The French were
experimenting with this technique after the French revolution, and Charles
Babbage had the insight that such simple mathematics could also be done
mechanically. His designs became the first mechanical computer. In a similar
way, supply chain leaders in low-cost countries are pointing to the current
software market and asking why they can't simply have the underlying process

executed with more human staff. We've yet to see a dominating off-the-shelf response to this challenge: clearly greater-than-human software for the supply chain visibility space. This would have huge potential in developed markets, but also the ability to penetrate new markets where low-cost labor is blocking the current generation of software. This is not a castle-in-the-sky dream. In other domains software has achieved exactly this level: greater than human performance so clear that systems are never compared to manual options. Even in the nearby spaces of EDI transmission and warehouse management systems running material handling equipment there can be no serious consideration of using "just more people." Hopefully the current vendors or new entrants to the supply chain visibility software market will set this as their goals for the future.

6

Build It Yourself ... In-House Visibility Software

In-house development has a mixed reputation. In some companies, it is the only option considered. Elsewhere there are horror stories about years lost due to poor quality systems developed by unqualified in-house staff. Earlier in the book several drivers were identified behind why in-house can be the right option in some circumstances. But the general IT industry sentiment in 2013 is that when all else is held equal, buying is better than building. For those who have strategic reasons to build their own software, this chapter reviews best practices on several key topics. It does not address all details, and especially leaves out general IT development considerations which affect any in-house development. If that level of background is needed, it is likely a warning sign that in-house development staff are not ready to do this kind of software anyway.

The Benefits of In-House Developed Solutions

There are market options available for supply chain visibility, so a company that decides to build its own solution would need to have compelling benefits that cannot be otherwise captured. Here is a review of some known and accepted benefits for building supply chain visibility technology in-house. These mainly relate to quality of solution, cost to deploy or maintain, and competitive differentiation.

BETTER INDUSTRY FIT

Some sectors or industries are not well served by existing market solutions. For example, military or governmental organizations would likely be unsatisfied by various aspects of off-the-shelf or SaaS solutions. The deficits appear in several places, such as feature scope, since the underlying decisions being modeled and how they are interrupted using the supply chain visibility solution are quite different from other industry sectors. At present there are several well targeted industry sectors, and perhaps another ten with only one market solution. That still leaves many supply chain owners left with no real pre-existing products to purchase.

BETTER REGIONAL FIT

There are severe regional differences in availability of off-the-shelf options. The most developed countries are also the most covered, which makes intuitive sense. But that won't help supply chain leaders elsewhere. Scrupulous buyers also realize that the lack of coverage is more about the professional services which are needed for a successful rollout. Buying a license to the software may be possible from Senegal, but who will train the local staff, run first line support in local dialects and working hours, and consult on the integration or configuration approach?

LOWER COST

As a general rule, in-house development will not offer a high probability of being lower cost for the same quality and timeline. But if we set aside the prejudices against internal development as a category and analyze the options on a case-by-case basis, it appears some supply chain visibility applications can be developed in-house at lower cost. One way the costs can be lower has to do with "right sizing" the solution. Market options will never be a perfect fit, meaning some features will go unused or will have to be developed expressly for a single customer's deployment. Both of those deviations in product scope are incrementally expensive. As an example, licensing a piece of supply chain software may cost $500,000 USD, and then to make two technical modifications to it may cost another $300,000 USD. The modifications become a proportionally large contributor to the total cost of ownership. Scope right-sizing also applies to intensity of usage. Current SaaS offerings are much lower cost for low-intensity business usage. As intensity of usage increases, such as number of transactions or full-time users, the costs match and then quickly surpass the cost of in-house development for the same scope. But, again, lowering cost is usually not achieved by building a new solution in-house.

COMPETITIVE DIFFERENTIATION

Imagine a company has created a secret tool it uses to get its products to the market before the competition. It involves business correspondence which can be digitalized and transmitted electronically. Let's call it "email." It's going to be the company's key competitive differentiation in the market: the way they will win. If that sounds crazy keep in mind that many organizations purchase supply chain visibility software with the same approach as their stated purpose. They assume the software will get them to market faster, lower inventory risks, save sales, or generally differentiate them from competitors. But the software itself is available to anyone, including their competitors. As delusional as this sounds, its commonplace.

Even if it costs more money, takes longer to deploy, or inflates the assets on the balance sheet, the temptation to purchase solutions from the market is in contradiction to a strategy of using them to differentiate a company from competitors. Realistically, most companies do not use visibility as a true differentiator. But key sectors, like logistics providers or 4PL firms, may compete based on this technology. Building custom visibility software (if done very well) creates a stronger barrier against competitors in the market.

HIGH CRITICALITY OF BUSINESS

The criticality of business need refers to how impactful a failure of the visibility application would be to the business. Failures come in different forms, for example data loss is one failure but a lost connection for 24 hours would be another. In most situations, visibility to the supply chain is not considered mission-critical to the company. But some businesses will depend enormously on the visibility software as an input to its business decisions.

Market options tend to offer good dependability and security for most business cases. But in-house development can always surpass them along an arbitrary dimension, such as ensured up-time or security. In some situations an in-house developed solution is required (or preferred) in order to ensure these levels of support for critical business decision making.

But criticality of business is relatively rare for supply chain visibility. As a practitioner interviewee noted:

> It may be important, but it's neither mission-critical nor a competitive differentiator. Apple will not outsource their design, for example, because it is both mission-critical and competitive differentiating. But supply chain visibility is not in the same category (Lienhard, Appendix A).

Another interviewee had similar sentiments:

> *Take Dell for example, they grew and competed through a direct-to-consumer offering and part of that service was visibility to the build-up of a customer's specific order. For other companies who are using make-to stock, deliver-from stock, this kind of visibility is not necessarily needed. At the end, if visibility is a core aspect of your business it should be held in-house. If visibility is not mission critical or a competitive differentiator, it should be acquired from outside (Karel, Appendix A).*

Overview of What to Build

The structure of the supply chain visibility software depends greatly on the kind of supply chain visibility needed by the business. By far the most critical components are:

1.   The data model, meaning the objects and how they relate to each other.

2.   The user interface, i.e. "the screens."

3.   The native support for interfaces to other applications, especially external to your company.

If in-house developed software gets these three things right in the first release, the visibility solution has a strong chance of success. If the in-house developed software gets them wrong, workarounds will be difficult for the users and one would see overall low grades on the supply chain visibility scorecard. The following section outlines generic data models for the major types of visibility and points out some important aspects of their architectures.

DATA MODEL EXAMPLE: TRACK AND TRACE FOR RETAIL

Retail track and trace requires a data model with strong order and item master support. The data model's mission is primarily to connect the planner's or buyer's data objects to the data objects used during material movements. The objects which planners may begin with include forecasts, budgets, blanket orders, purchase orders, season codes, supplier codes, style codes, destination (i.e. region, country, city, retail store) or item numbers. The data model then needs to link these starting points to the details about where the materials are and when they are expected at the point of sale. The data model shown below can support this kind of visibility. A couple of important points:

1. The forecast or budget object can reference other forecasts or budgets. For example an annual budget is referenced by a quarterly budget, which is referenced by the monthly budget. Forecasts or budgets in retail organizations are often matrixed, such as a forecast per store, but also a forecast per season or per style.

2. The item master has a similar self-referencing relationship as the forecast or budget object. Items tend to aggregate into product families. As an example, a specific jacket may be part of a set, which is part of a style, which is part of a season, which is part of a line.

3. The organization master allows the visibility of aggregate business activity for a given business partner. It would include suppliers, but also transporters, agents, inspection companies, and so forth. When these are connected to the other objects it needs to be done through a "role" attribute. So a company like "UPS" may be linked to a shipment as the "transporter" role, and "Fun Shirt Shenzhen factory" may be linked to the same shipment as a "Supplier" role.

4. It's tempting to connect PO lines directly to shipments, but this can diverge too much from the physical material flow. Loads (or something similar like a booking, Forwarders Cargo Receipt, ASN, and so forth) provide good flexibility to keep materials grouped according to how the supplier shipped them, while also supporting consolidated shipments as a single object.

5. If there are multiple legs, with consolidation or deconsolidation occurring in-between, the load object remains intact but is assigned to different shipments at different times. The "N:N" between loads and shipment in the diagram is indicating that at any one time, a load should be on one shipment but that over its life the relationship between load and shipment can be multiple-to-multiple. This is analogous to "spouse count" in most countries where polygamy is illegal, where a person can have many spouses during their life but only one at any given time.

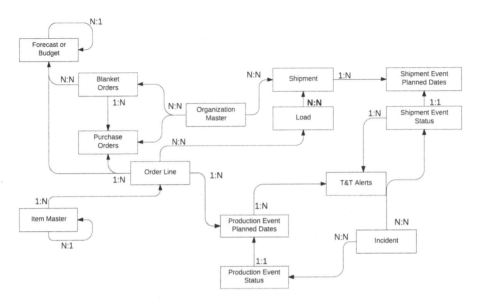

Figure 6.1 Data relation model template for track and trace visibility

DATA MODEL EXAMPLE: WORLD AS A WAREHOUSE

The world as a warehouse visibility approach benefits from very rich objects for describing materials and locations. The data model also needs to be geared towards high record count and transaction speed. The following relationship is the most important: unique material handling units should have encapsulation capabilities by other unique material handling units (UMHU). This makes business sense if we think about materials and how they are actually managed. A uniquely identified box gets added to a uniquely identified pallet. The pallet gets added to a uniquely identified sandwich pallet. Then the sandwich pallet gets added to a unique trailer. The trailer is put on to a double-trailer truck, and so forth. At any given point the encapsulation allows an event to be targeted at the top-most UMHU, which is also matching the physical reality. For example, the departure of the double-trailer truck is a truck-level event and not an event which is happening directly to all the truck content boxes. They are indeed departing as well, but only because they are consolidated into the truck. So the event happens to one UMHU and it propagates out to the other UMHUs contained within it.

What else is there of interest in the world as warehouse data model? One point is that it's viable to have long-lived or permanently circulating UMHUs. For example, a company may ship the same re-usable tote or industrial carnet

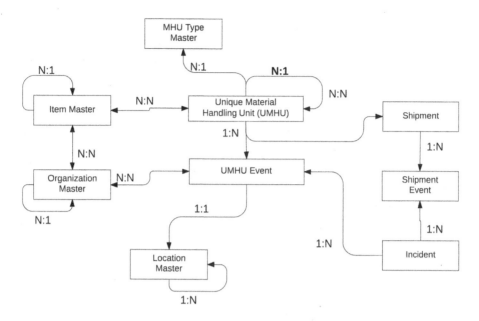

Figure 6.2   **Data relation model template for world as a warehouse visibility**

a hundred times with different products for each shipment. These are the same UMHUs, but contain different things at different times. Ocean containers are a classic example of this behavior, and something which has broken a large number of in-house developed visibility systems during acceptance testing. The reference between UMHUs to MHU types is an optional aspect. If strict control of material handling unit will be done based on what type of MHU it is, then this makes sense. An alternative is to support tagging, thereby enabling description of UMHU types without master-data enforcement. The last remark is that a no-SQL database approach may be beneficial if high transaction scale is expected and where it's unlikely (because of the physical nature of the goods) that a single record will be attempted to be updated by many sites or users at once. No-SQL won't guarantee ACID database processing but will guarantee eventual consistency, and in most cases of the world as warehouse model the improved scaling and speed would be considered a viable tradeoff.

DATA MODEL: THE EVENT MANAGER

The data model for an event manager style supply chain visibility software is going to be a beast. While it shouldn't become a supply chain planning application, the presence of plans and their related data drive up the minimum complexity. An event manager model begins with some kind of plan. The plan object can be on many levels, such as capacity, production, raw material orders, finished goods orders, sales, inventory, and so forth. What these have in common is a sense of time-based dependency where a series of expected events for the given object are distributed across time, and the supply chain visibility software makes the impacts of events in the start of that timeline visible for estimated events later in that timeline. Business goals might also include seeing big-picture affects, such as total impact on available-to-promise women's wear in a certain season or style or region due to a typhoon in southern China. As with the world-as-a-warehouse type visibility, the design struggle is getting the data captured at the right granularity and with the right population of object types. Once that happens, valuable aggregation can occur through reporting or business intelligence systems. There can be more than one plan object, and these are the right discovery questions to consider when estimating the complexity of the resulting model:

1.   How many plan objects should be covered?

2.   Are the plans linked causally, i.e. does a change in one plan need to cause an automated change in another plan object?

3.   How complex is the relationship between the plan objects?

The most daunting requirements would be a large number of plan objects, linked in complex, causal, multiple-to-multiple relationships. But of course the resulting supply chain visibility software is then likely to be more valuable. The model shown below depicts a situation where there are three plans, with simple but causal relationships. The connectors indicate the plan-to-plan relationships but these are often complex, and the rounded boxes show where (highly configurable) business rule engines would need to operate. An example user story would be something like this:

1.   A user changes the bill of processes for an existing product, perhaps increasing its required quality checking steps.

2.   That change propagates via the purchase orders to revise the amount of projected process capacity needed along the production plan's timeline at specific locations.

3.   The increase capacity requirements trigger an evaluation of the business rules for how this should update related sales plans.

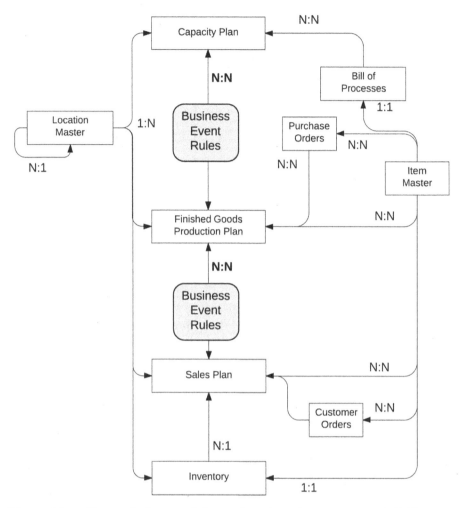

Figure 6.3   Data relation model template for event manager visibility

4.   The entire scope of business is available for reporting: planned capacity, capacity committed to production of goods, and planned sales of those goods.

DATA MODEL: MOBILE DECISION MAKING

Mobile decision making via supply chain visibility requires an architecture that is ready to deal with spatial coordinates. Spatial databases have some unique features which go beyond typical SQL relational databases. The Open Geospatial Consortium has a standard called "Simple Features," which

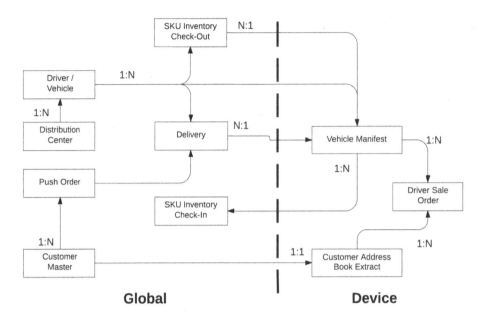

Figure 6.4   **Data relation model template for mobile decision support visibility**

should be used as a starting point. This addresses both expanded capabilities and performance optimization, since standard indexing approaches will not perform well with queries based on distances or other spatial aspects. The other critical data model issue with mobile decision-making type visibility is to decide if it will leverage thin-client or thick-client architecture. Thin-client will make it more agile in adopting new mobile-device capabilities as they come to the marketplace, since it makes fewer assumptions about the device. The advantages of thick-client appear when the solution requires periodic operation in an un-tethered mode, i.e. asynchronous operations. For obvious reasons a thick-client approach requires two data models, one for the central application and one for the local device.

The data model below covers a very basic driver-managed-inventory visibility solution. For example, it would cover drivers who do both planned "push" orders and also carry stock for on-site sales. It uses a thick-client approach where data is persisted to the driver's device so that they can work in areas or weather conditions that do not allow constant connectivity. The dashed line shows the data model in both its global context, and what parts are replicated to the mobile device.

DATA MODEL: SAVE THE SALE

The architecture for "save the sale" style supply chain visibility is focused on matching supply with demand. A more detailed analysis shows that sales are "saved" by being able to fulfill them using inventory that is somewhere else in the supply chain. In order to do the matching job well, the visibility model needs to have fairly comprehensive coverage of both the supply objects (blanket orders, production orders, and so forth) and the demand objects (point of sale capacity, point of sale inventory, and so forth).

So, what are the main aspects of this architecture? The first is that it tracks physical inventory per point of sale (and it's often assumed that forward DCs would count as points of sale). But, in addition to physical inventory, it also has dedicated objects to track "Available to Promise" (ATP) inventory. The ATP inventory is a kind of virtual stockroom or store shelf, comprised of all products which can be used in a sale via a specific point of sale, and for a specific customer. The customer could in fact be a customer segment, rather than a named person, depending on the business. The point of sale could also be a combination of location (such as a mall kiosk or web store shopping cart) along with the desired service level (delivered today, delivered next week, and so forth). Properly administered, this gives a powerful foundation for dynamically pooling and distributing inventory (both physical and virtual) on the basis of who is demanding it and via what point of purchase. In the diagram there are also some telltale signs of the complexity of modern retailing. For example a transaction can relate to multiple customers (a wedding gift registry, for example, which needs to relate transactions to both the buyer of the gift and the couple who selected a retailer as a gifting venue). Another example is the N:N relationship between a point of sale and a final sale transaction. Often the customers interact with several points of sale during their purchase, such as visiting the retailer's website before purchasing in the store (or vice versa).

The last point worth mentioning is the "Capacity Master" object in the middle. This hides a lot of subtle limitations regarding feasible matches on supply and demand. Most points of sale have working hours, limits on where they can ship to, etc. On top of this are limits on how fast products can be moved physically, the total throughput ability of the facilities which must process them, and business rules regarding everything from minimum shippable quantity to the size of a retail store's stockroom. Taken together, these can be encapsulated in a generic "capacity" object which indicates limitations on what inventory is promised for a potential sale along independent dimensions.

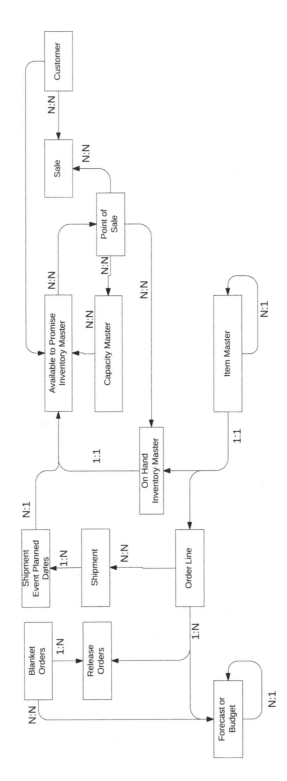

Figure 6.5   Data relation model template for save the sale visibility

DATA MODEL: SERIAL AND LOT NUMBER TRACKING

Tracking of serial numbers or lot numbers requires tight control of the relationship between products and their material handling units. For businesses with one product in one material handling unit, this is superfluous. But generally life is not so simple. Even if the business starts or ends with a simple MHU to product relationship, during the supply chain lifecycle the MHUs can be more complex at intermediary points. Because the serial number or lot number's lifecycle only ends when the product is sold and also consumed, the objects covered by this form of supply chain distribution should extend past the customer sale event. For example, if the product is a computer that has a warranty and might be sent back for repair, this event should be part of the visibility information. It's also common to incorporate additional objects, like shipments and shipment events, and these connect naturally to the MHU or the MHU events.

Attentive readers might notice that this looks like an alternative version of the "World as a Warehouse" data model. That is correct, to the extent that both models are primarily concerned with tightly controlling the physical flow of materials. But, the lot and serial number tracking data model extends this by

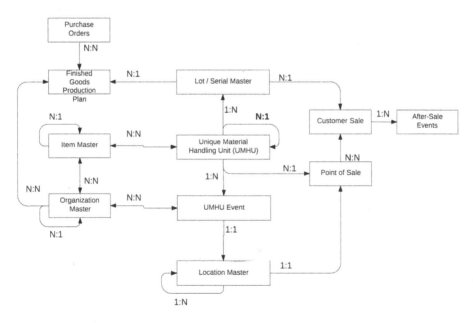

Figure 6.6   **Data relation model template for lot number and serial number visibility**

relating physical materials to key production attributes, and then continuing the scope beyond the point where materials are sold to when they are completely consumed.

Building the User Interface

The graphic user interface, or "GUI," is often the weakest aspect of in-house supply chain visibility software development. One reason is that aesthetic experience is considered a low priority when the application doesn't have to be "sold" to the users. Second, most organizations do not have large enough IT departments to employ a professional usability engineer in the development teams. Of course those engineers can be hired as contractors or consultants, but this limits their involvement in the core solution decisions and also makes their part of the budget particularly susceptible to being cut.

A weak GUI tends to drag down the perceived power and value of the application. The users have a gut-level reaction to working with aesthetically or operationally flawed interfaces. The user's reaction is important even if they can be "forced" to use the application, because many tasks depend on things like user engagement. It also influences the perceived quality of the decision support, and hence the trustworthiness of the decisions being made. The GUI is also not judged in a vacuum, but alongside other enterprise or web applications. In particular there is a trend that indicates business software will be critiqued on terms of consumer software's aesthetics and usability. That means the accounting software will be compared by users to their Facebook or Google experiences, not to other enterprise software that they use. This is a real and important trend, leading towards higher standards for minimal acceptable GUIs.

Entire books are available which cover the GUI design and implementation, so it's not appropriate to try to cover those topics here. In-house development teams can do research on this topic elsewhere and then adopt a GUI style that is readily understandable to industry users or make an intentional deviation if they believe other formats are more productive.

7

Borrowing Supply Chain Visibility

This chapter examines a major option available to most supply chain managers in their search for supply chain visibility: the option to get visibility services as a perk of working with a given logistics service provider. Sometimes the visibility service has a nominal charge but most times it is offered for free so long as the logistics provider is being paid for related services such as buying agency, transport, consolidation, or regional coordination. Although there are companies who do not provide logistics services that have visibility solution offerings, the rest of the chapter focuses just on visibility as a perk from a logistics service provider.

Logistics providers occupy a broad range of service niches around the more specific act of holding materials or transporting materials from place to place. The industry terminology reflects this situation. Transport companies in traditional configurations as asset-operators and mode-specific will be referred to as a "carrier" or a "trucker." Asset-light or multi-modal transport companies get names like "third party logistics" or the acronym "3PL." And those whose focus is on human resources or in/outsourcing identify as lead logistics provider or "4PL," referring to a fourth party position to the actual transportation of materials. More terms are sure to come as nuances and niches develop in this sector. But, regardless of naming or strategic focus, all major logistics service providers have instituted some form of supply chain visibility as part of their service offering. It is widely considered a minimum offering in order to compete for even second rate customers, and logistics service providers (hereafter simply called "LSPs") tend to find the topic of supply chain visibility frustrating. The frustration is rooted in the ambivalent definition of visibility among practitioners and how the market treats visibility provided by LSPs. Below we examine these points in more detail.

First, note that visibility is a kind of emergent result, a consequence of a process, rather than a specific checklist like ISO quality standards. This leads to wide variation in visibility solutions: there are no visibility standards in the industry. For LSPs, this has turned into a no-win situation; they do not get the benefits of standardization (lower risk, lower cost to build and operate) while also unable to charge premiums for differentiated solutions. The LSPs who provide visibility tend to provide it in vastly different ways, sometimes to such an extent it's not clear that two LSPs can be compared side by side in regards to their visibility offering. Sometimes, an LSP has a clearly better fit in how it targets and delivers visibility for a given prospective customer. Other times, two LSPs provide different but equally satisfactory visibility for a prospect and the competition hinges on other areas. More often than either of these situations is that two or more LSPs offer different and un-equal visibility solutions and the prospective customer must make a strategic-focus decision about which kind of visibility is more beneficial. One LSP may offer much better up-stream visibility at origins, while their competitors can surpass them in downstream visibility in destination markets. Ultimately this pressures the LSPs to make investments in either closing competitive gaps of visibility execution or to become better at technical sales based on their unique approach to the topic. Neither of these investments is particularly sustainable, from a competitive perspective, and neither enables higher margins with most of their customers. The core of frustration behind all this competition among LSPs over visibility is that it offers very few direct benefits to the winning LSP. Among the logistics community it's well known that business may be lost by an LSP over visibility, but is not often won only by the visibility. And even when business is secured in part due to visibility services, those services come as a free add-on to the other for-fee services. In other words, visibility is seen as a free perk of being a customer of a given LSP.

The second, and perhaps more pernicious, issue which frustrates LSPs as regards their visibility offering is the dichotomy of requirements they receive from prospective customers. When an LSP approaches a small to midsized prospect the expectations around supply chain visibility are completely different than when approaching a larger sized prospect. In a word, we could explain the difference by saying that larger companies are looking for *compliance* from their LSPs. Larger companies tend to have a well-defined, centrally managed, proprietary visibility solution which they expect the LSP to plug into via electronic data feeds. The larger the company, the more likely it is to have enough mass to support a supply chain analyst team who has built this kind of visibility approach. To these large companies and their supply chain management staff, *consistency* between LSPs is much more valuable than letting them focus on their individual visibility strengths. The consistency means, among other things, less work to combine their data into a holistic picture, less lock-in risk to one provider, and more strategic control over where to take visibility in the future. So the larger companies establish their visibility process or system and expect the LSPs it selects to comply with its requirements. For the LSP, the situation has very few upsides. First, they commoditize themselves and make it easier to be switched out by a competitor. The visibility services become something which can lose the large customer, but can never win the customer or extract higher revenue. Meeting each large customer's requirements means developing different aspects of the LSP's visibility service to an externally controlled standard, something which requires investments in IT and staff. The demands of these large companies often do not overlap; they are too finely tuned to the needs of the individual situation to be of general use. So the LSP's operation doesn't reap broad strategic advantages along the lines of "rising tides lift all boats." To the contrary, meeting a large customer's demands may dominate the budget of an LSP and leave them under-capitalized for their general visibility offering. Finally, the role of the LSP tends to be secondary rather than primary in the visibility setup, which is how the customer wants it in order to have the power to swap out the LSP quickly. But another result of being supportive rather than in real control is that the LSP cannot bring these visibility setups to their smaller customers, even if those customers would be willing to pay a premium for them. In other words, an LSP who serves Apple cannot replicate the Apple supply chain visibility with other, smaller, customers even though it is making significant investments to support the Apple visibility systems and processes.

Taken together, this paints a picture of LSPs as:

1.   Almost always offering supply chain visibility.

2.   Offering different variations of supply chain visibility.

3.   Focusing on compliance to the demands of large companies.

4.   Often giving the visibility away at no cost, as a perk of being a customer.

Point three from the list above also means supply chain visibility is often a "loss leading" service, meaning it directly reduces the profitability of the LSP but with the intention to indirectly increase revenue and therefore potentially profit (in absolute value).

Early Successes with LSP Visibility

Probably the root of supply chain visibility services from LSPs was the rise in the USA of parcel carriers such as FedEx and UPS using multi-point package barcode scanning during the parcel delivery lifecycle. When this first appeared it was broadly criticized by other LSPs as a tremendously costly investment which provided little or no value to the customer. There was incredulousness at the idea that customers wanted to go on to a slow internet connection, type in a serialized tracking ID, and view where their package was scanned at along various points in time. But those critics were missing an important technology inflection point as it happened. The exponential spread of cheap, reliable, and good-enough internet connections lowered the barriers to customers trying such a service. Once a customer tried it, especially the kind of customers who were already paying high per-parcel rates for expedited and time-committed deliveries, the world would never be the same. The early adopters of this supply chain visibility were companies sending a relatively low volume of time-sensitive parcels. A much larger volume of customers for parcel track and trace arrived with the dot-com bubble and the need to earn consumer trust over a new shopping channel.

The LSP community was right in some respects: scanning every parcel seven to 15 times over its lifecycle of only a few days was an expensive system to setup. The earliest of adopters, like FedEx and UPS, needed to hire industrial engineers, IT specialists, and invest in very expensive servers, radio frequency scanning devices, fixed scanning devices, and a host of other technologies. As was obvious in the table on patents for supply chain visibility, UPS invested heavily in the 2000s to build these technologies. But their return was not just about sustaining premium pricing for parcel deliveries. The rich data provided by all this scanning was also used in process and facility design. It eventually led to orders of magnitude better quality, consistency, and productivity. An example of this is the "worldport" facility operated by UPS in Louisville, Kentucky, USA. The facility is extremely automated and depends totally on the standards and presence of barcoded labels of each package coming through the facility.

Early Success and Recent Frustrations

Supply chain managers evaluating their LSPs or potential LSPs as a source of supply chain visibility should go into the situation with some skepticism. Asset-based LSPs control large parts of the physical supply chain, and non-asset based LSPs contract with or coordinate asset operators over even larger portions of the physical supply chain. In theory, it's reasonable to assume that they should be good at data collection during these physical activities. In practice, LSPs generally prove less capable in data stewardship than in logistics execution. One industry practitioner who was interviewed noted:

> Our recent 3PL Study reveals that the major frustration between Shippers and 3PLs lays in the lacking visibility. Hence, there is still a lot of improvement possible particularly if you think about the new technologies allowing mobile, anywhere access to data (Karel, Appendix A).

Some of the frequent complaints among supply chain managers regarding LSP performance of supply chain visibility include:

- Poor data quality (timeliness, consistency, completeness, and breadth).

- Inability or no commitment to integrate data from and to other sources.

- Poor tools for sense-making of the data.

- Poor re-integration of the visibility insights into decision making.

These four criticisms align to the four steps in the supply chain visibility process. In other words, LSPs are criticized for being poor in all the steps which produce supply chain visibility. This contrasts starkly with the early successes from parcel carriers based in the USA and their adoption of barcode scanning over the parcel lifecycle. Probably the most compelling aspect of the current LSP supply chain visibility solutions is just that they are offered for free as a perk of being a customer.

There is a frustrating gap between the early successes of parcel tracking and later disappointments in LSP visibility. But the gap has logical roots. First, the growth of parcel scan and track services were competitive differentiators for the parcel companies investing in them. Early-adopter clients made it clear that they would make a buying decision on these features and pay higher prices for them. Later, during the rise of ecommerce and the dot-com bubble in the USA, even mainstream customers who had not participated in the bleeding edge period were willing to pay premiums for the detailed tracking services. The revenue lift was substantial. For example, a carrier like UPS could charge several US dollars more per package in the consumer segment for the traceability during the late 1990s and early 2000s. For the parcel carriers, the revenue was also being supplemented by cost reduction programs which leveraged the immense pool of parcel scan data to support process and industrial site engineering. Between the cost reduction, competitive differentiation, and increased price points for services, early visibility services were well worth their investments for the parcel carriers. Unfortunately, extending that success outwards proved too difficult.

First, expansion of even parcel tracking in a geographic sense was costly and prone to failure. As mentioned earlier, the earliest adoption was only in the USA. Other markets came later or not at all. The second wave of customers in the US was e-commerce sites during the dot-com bubble. A similar wave of customer demand and revenue potential did not materialize in other markets where internet penetration was still too low. Even in 2005 to 2010 in major markets with high internet and ecommerce penetration like the UK, the smaller size geographically meant that transport had much less variability and the overall value of in-transit confirmations was less than in the USA.

The second reason why the LSP community found it challenging to expand parcel scan and track visibility outward to other logistics businesses was the lack of market interest in paying premiums for those new services. Whereas the parcel carriers were adding line-itemed charges for their visibility, LSPs in areas like freight forwarding, reverse logistics, local deliveries, and origin consolidation were unable to sustain separate pricing. In part, this should give potential customers pause for thought anyway: we always get what we pay for. When the supply chain manager negotiates an LSP down to no revenue for the use of their technology and to deploying the technology as a commodity so it can be switched out quickly, all the motivation to make that visibility solution into something great has been eroded. Visibility as a perk is no free lunch. In terms of quality, after visibility became a perk it lost the market force driving its refinement within the LSP community. Not only were LSPs not getting paid for their visibility investments, there is also not much internal improvements being driven using the wealth of visibility data. Visibility came to be seen as client-facing, and a give-away, rather than a potential leverage point for industrial engineering of the internal operations of each LSP.

Underlying Technology

A supply chain manager who is considering leveraging an LSP for their supply chain visibility should take time to investigate the LSP's underlying technology.

As discussed previously in the book, supply chain visibility is not just technology but really a process. Notwithstanding, technology plays a crucial role in executing that process. The market trend today is for LSPs to fall into three categories regarding their technology strategy for supply chain visibility:

1.   In-house software, tied in to proprietary hardware such as high volume material handling equipment or cross-dock RFID or barcode readers.

2.   Third party software with little or no modifications.

3.   Third party software which is heavily modified, or weaved into a "best of breed" software suite such that visibility really is the product of many equally leveraged systems.

Technology trends are easily reversed, but as of 2013 the logistics service sector seems to favor the third option shown above. In-house developed systems are particularly out of favor among most LSPs. The smallest of LSPs may have in-house systems (often developed by contractor software development houses) simply to reduce the total cost of ownership. But these LSPs barely qualify to compete against more established LSPs, and certainly won't be winning based on their visibility offering.

Larger LSPs who are noteworthy for using their own visibility systems include Kuehne & Nagel, DAMCO, UPS, and OOCL logistics. In all of these situations the LSP's value propositions are tightly dependent on their visibility technology offering. All of these companies are above industry average, and DAMCO and Kuehne & Nagel are really stand-out leaders in the spaces they compete. In market-facing messages, the positioning of these companies is that they have more superior field expertise than supply chain software vendors, and can mobilize similarly qualified development teams to implement on their plans. Without the ability to conduct detailed reviews, it would be hard to say if these systems are truly superior to market options. But it seems clear that they are at least better integrated into the operations of the LSP's business. Since visibility is a culmination of a process involving- but not limited to-technology, the net result is that these three companies produce better visibility using their in-house systems.

In contrast to the smallest LSPs and the leaders like DAMCO and Kuehne & Nagel, most LSPs in the market are using a combination of third party software integrated into a tapestry of systems. For example, companies like DHL and Agility deploy both GT Nexus and Log-Net for supply chain visibility depending on the location and the client needs. Panalpina leverages Manhattan Associates' EEM, Log-Net, AX4 from AXIT, and sends data feeds into GT Nexus. DB Schenker has an in-house developed system called C2C but also uses GT Nexus. Even DAMCO deploys a mix of in-house systems and an optimization system derived from Llamasoft. As an indicative statistic, in a study on the state of supply chain visibility software in 2012, 950 out of 2000 software implementations from the main global vendors were for LSPs (Cap Gemini, 2012). This shows the extent to which:

1.   LSPs are expected to have visibility solutions; and

2.   that they prefer to buy off the shelf software and integrate it with their other systems.

Although it may seem that having multiple systems is a cost burden, in several ways it is a prudent approach for the LSP. First, it prevents them from being locked in with a single technology provider. Regardless of their acquisition diligence and expertise, larger LSPs would face serious risk if their only visibility technology provider were to become insolvent or simply fail to keep up with the latest developments. LSPs also have the chance to cover more use-cases in supply chain visibility by having multiple systems to choose from. This is why companies like Panalpina, with its large portfolio of visibility technologies, tend to do well with exacting and complex customers who fall outside the standards of most other providers. Lastly, having multiple visibility systems to offer a prospective client is a way to nullify a potentially competitive differentiator. A competitor who approached a prospective customer with GT Nexus as their visibility solution is then neutralized in terms of visibility offering, returning the competitive factors to other areas where the LSP may feel stronger. Of course, this leads to visibility being a commodity and to the fact it is treated as a free perk instead of a paid service. But for LSPs who might otherwise lose all the revenue from a deal, it's a reasonable response.

Finally, a very small number of LSPs go to market with a third party system ... but really just one. This is the "all eggs, one basket" strategy. Lower in cost, it still is not a common thing in the LSP industry. Carriers like Matson Navigation, for example, are large enough to need to offer a visibility solution but don't see that as a primary competitive aspect of their service. So they use GT Nexus and nothing else. If an account really needs another kind of visibility, such as case-level tracking, then the opportunity is lost but perhaps wasn't going to work out anyway.

What does this means for the supply chain manager who is evaluating the option of getting supply chain visibility as a perk from their LSP? Realistically any technology approach has its benefits and risks. In the context of an LSP providing visibility services, the technology is being multiplied by the process it's embedded in. A highly engineered process can achieve great visibility even with mediocre underlying technology. An example is the UPS visibility offering. Their system, called Flex Global View, had started life developed in-house by the Fritz forwarding company before being acquired by UPS. It was acceptable but not market-leading as a stand-alone software. That said, the overall engineering culture at UPS lead to a superior visibility offering because once the technology was properly tuned in to the UPS processes the synergistic effects were large. In the same way that a fighter jet is useless without the best pilots, visibility technology won't carry a poorly designed or executed process. Several of the industry practitioner interviews noted that LSPs should be uniquely poised to marry visibility with other processes, and therefore are the logical partner to carry the torch for supply chain visibility technologies. One interviewee stated this view as:

> *The core competence of an LSP is to provide operational excellence in supply chain movements including the required visibility. Even though the IT gap is still significant, i.e. what shippers are expecting and what LSPs are offering (see Cap Gemini's 3PL Study), I believe long-term 3PLs will be more integrated in those processes as the industry is trying to close the gaps and in addition are moving in more supply chain related domains (Karel, Appendix A).*

Strengths and Weaknesses: How to Evaluate Visibility as a Perk

To wrap up this chapter, we'll look specifically at how to evaluate an LSP's visibility offering from the perspective of a supply chain manager who is a prospective customer. The steps suggested here should tie-in easily to the usual buying cycle performed for any significant sourcing of enterprise services. In summary, these steps are suggested:

1. Based on the maturity of the business and its unique needs and resources, decide what visibility capabilities or sub-processes should be outsourced to the LSP.

2. Evaluate the LSP as a pure logistics provider, without considering the visibility offering.

3.   Evaluate the underlying technology of the visibility offering,
      without consideration for the integration into the LSP's execution
      processes.

4.   Evaluate the marriage of process and technology demonstrated by
      the LSP in the visibility offering. Create a supply chain visibility
      scorecard for the decisions that should be supported by the visibility
      solution.

5.   Evaluate the strategic risks associated with this LSP: the walk-away
      risk (also sometimes called "stickiness") of relying on them for
      supply chain visibility. Consider realistic mitigation options and
      their costs.

The five steps described above should give a supply chain manager or a team
of analysts the proper perspective from which to make a strong case for or
against deriving visibility as a perk of working with an LSP. Step two is a due-
diligence exercise, which should be done first because the LSP is primarily
doing something else besides supply chain visibility. If they are not good
enough in their primary task, it makes little sense to consider them for the free
perk of visibility they are willing to throw in to sweeten the deal. Steps three
and four are focused on the visibility solution and its expected results. This is
where the supply chain visibility scorecard should be used. Steps one and five
are part of a strategic sourcing process, where the LSP is not evaluated directly,
but in comparison to other available options in the market. In effect, step five
is focused on the opportunity costs associated with using this LSP in a specific
configuration.

    The first step in this process is the one often skipped and which then
wreaks havoc in the decision-making team when an LSP must be selected. At
its most simple, this is a decision of whether to rely on one LSP for the majority
or totality of supply chain visibility, or to expect LSPs to be compliant with a
centralized process which is managed in-house. In other words: should the LSP
provide an entire visibility solution or just plug in data or specific deliverables
into an existing visibility solution? The answer to this question determines the
rest of the process, because it affects which LSPs are going to be evaluated
(most LSPs specialize in one or the other approach), what the LSP will be asked
to do, and how they will be evaluated for best-fit. As one industry practitioner
interviewee stated: "we need to ask 'what are the capabilities the company feels
are their core value adding activities.' This helps decides what parts are best
handled by partners or providers" (Wilcox, Apendix A).

Generally, smaller companies tend to find more value in having all or nearly all visibility done by one LSP, often in an arrangement where the LSP has nearly all the contract logistics volume as well. Larger companies who have more internal supply chain management resources tend to favor arrangements where the LSPs get smaller slices of the contract logistics budget and are forced to comply with specific visibility processes decided by the customer rather than the LSP. In between is a whole range of approaches which are perfect for a given company. Completing step one means that the decision-making group has formal commitments to:

1. How much business would be awarded to the LSP.

2. Which visibility tasks would be handled by the LSP (meaning budgeted, designed, executed, and so forth).

3. Which visibility tasks the company retains.

4. How long this split of business responsibilities should be maintained.

It's easy to see why these questions will simply come back up if they are skipped in the beginning. Later in the buying cycle, multiple LSPs may be considered "best" if the questions from step one are answered differently by different stakeholders. The chances of success are higher if the goals of the buying process are defined up front, often before emotions or politics get involved, rather than later.

8

Important Technological Trends

This chapter reviews five technologies that are likely to cause large changes to the domain of supply chain visibility. The technologies reviewed here are in the proof of concept or ramp-up phase as of 2013, so they should see early-adopter usage by 2016 and widespread usage by 2020. That timeline makes them perfect candidates for discussion here, because the feasibility of the technologies is already proven and while the costs or scalability are being optimized it is up to the supply chain practitioner community to decide how they are used. With these technologies, there really are no best practices (yet), but by the end of the decade there will be. Of course, some of them may never become widely adopted, either because a reliable usage pattern never emerges or because newer technologies leap-bound them the way wireless networks leaped landline telephony in much of the world. But there is a high probability that most or all of them will achieve widespread use and therefore radically alter supply chain visibility as it is practiced today.

Before going into the details on these technology trends, let's look at what makes them qualified to be singled out as important inflection-points for supply chain visibility. All of the five trends are a kind of "trailing edge" technology, which means that they have their most important impacts as the cumulative usage base reaches a critical mass. In other words, these technology areas won't change the field of supply chain management when a formal proof is made in academic settings, or even by early adopters among supply chain leaders. These technology areas will induce inflection points in supply chain visibility when they achieve mass adoption. To paraphrase Clay Shirky: Communication tools don't get interesting until they get technologically boring.

Now on to the technology trends. They are listed on the next page and then discussed in detail one at a time:

1.   The maker movement.

2.   The internet of things.

3.   Machine-Human symbiosis.

4.   Machine learning.

5.   Big data.

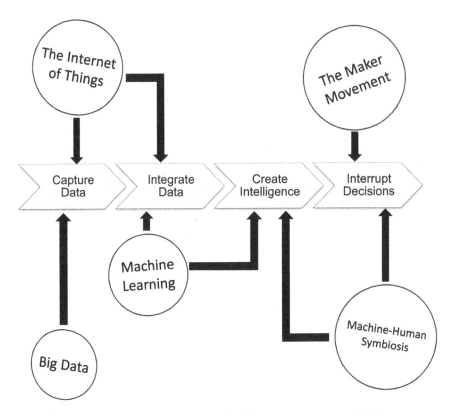

Figure 8.1   Critical technology trends likely to impact visibility

The Maker Movement

The maker movement is an emerging community, primarily among hobbyist, focused on distributed manufacturing and its related cultural, business, and aesthetic impacts. One of the common components of the maker movement is the appearance of hacker spaces, also sometimes called FabLabs, where flexible manufacturing tools are available for use on a membership or rental basis. These facilities enable creativity and individualistic design which can be harnessed as either a prototyping phase for later large-scale production or as small-batch finished-goods production at costs which are not yet competitive with much larger volume production. There are many roots to the movement, some of them hobbyist and some industrial, but the current state of the community is characterized by an appreciation for the uniqueness of individual expression over standard mass production. For example, 3D printing is a common tool used in the maker movement, but the community tends to prefer to see the tool (3D printing) as subservient to the maker (the designer). The maker movement is very widespread geographically, and is not a regional phenomenon.

The maker movement has many important parallels with the personal computing revolution which took place in the 1970s and 1980s. During those decades the personal computer was a hobbyist pursuit, in large part without a compelling narrative for how it added value to the average person (or business). In the 1970s and 1980s the personal computer was an example of the trailing edge of information processing. Anyone who owned an early IBM or Atari personal computer had no chance of competing in direct competition with the best computers being deployed in business, academic, and military settings. Nonetheless, the trailing edge became the dominant story because its low cost, wide deployment, and freedom for individual creativity lead to incredible value being created. So it appears to be with the maker movement right now. The bright and lucky children of the 1970s and 1980s were toying with their parent's home computers, learning early coding languages along the way. Today they are toying with distributed manufacturing technologies like synthetic biology or 3D printing, and what they will produce in adulthood may be equally impactful to supply chain visibility.

The maker movement's relation to supply chain management is in its nurturing and demonstration of the potential of distributed manufacturing. Distributed manufacturing has three specific disruptive impacts on supply chains in their current form. First, it redefines the geographic landscape of where business should be done. Second, it changes the optimal quantity to be brought to market. Third, it reduces the minimum cycle time to respond with product changes or bring new products to market. These are addressed in more detail individually below, and then their impacts on supply chain visibility are discussed.

Redefining the Geography of Production

Distributed manufacturing has the potential to radically alter the importance of geography in supply chains. The current approach to arranging supply chains geographically is that there are three poles or points to which the supply chain must be anchored. These points are the point of demand, the point of production, and the point of raw materials. For a large apparel brand bringing designer jeans to market, for example, they are anchored to the USA for cotton, South-east Asia for production steps, and the USA and Europe for demand. Naively we assume that the point of production is optimized for human labor costs. But for many products this is not strictly true. As an example, consider the Apple iPhone. In 2012, the television channel ABC visited Foxconn (the manufacturer for almost all iPhones in 2012) and reported that average labor costs in its Shenzhen factory were $1.78 USD per hour for the assembly workers. Various estimates correlate the full labor cost embedded in each iPhone to be between $13 and $30 USD. But the cost estimate of the components being assembled in each iPhone is $180 to $190 USD. In other words, the labor input to a product like an iPhone is simply not worth optimizing when compared to the direct coordination, production assets, and financing of components. Other evidence points in the same direction. The Shenzhen site where many iPhones are produced is in fact a large campus, where nearly 300,000 workers live on-site. Within a few miles are similarly large campuses for most of the suppliers who feed in machine parts, glass, and other components for the assembly work. The co-location of all this specialized production capability is actually what is being optimized for, rather than labor costs. Obviously there are lower wage areas than Shenzhen China, but those locations are not co-located within a manufacturing ecosystem which could support the assembly process. Spreading out the production points adds transport costs, complexity of coordination, capital tied up in raw materials or component stock, and finally time to market.

Where the maker movement and distributed manufacturing comes into this picture is in the growth of multi-purpose facilities which are designed for flexibility instead of efficiency. Rather than a site which produces a small number of parts but at incredible volumes, the influence of distributed manufacturing is for sites to be designed for producing the widest possible array of products, even if the flexibility results in lower maximum output. A distributed manufacturing approach to the iPhone would be to produce them in low quantities around the world in sites which can execute all of the steps between raw materials or basic components up to the finished product. While this may seem far-fetched with a product with its design as well guarded as the iPhone, a strong case could be made that the personal printing technologies of the 1980s and 1990s were the precursors to the local, perhaps even personal, manufacturing of nearly all physical products.

It's overlooked today, but as recently as the 1960s and 1970s publishing was an industrial art. People studied or apprenticed to learn about fonts, kerning, margins, line spacing, and so forth. With the advent of personal publishing, first of nearly pure text and later of graphical design and layout, these became part of the normal scope of many professional's skill repertoire. It's not that the industrial art of graphic design disappeared, but that it became drastically less concentrated because the majority of total printing migrated towards the general public. In a similar way, distributed manufacturing has the potential to allow anyone to click a "build" button the same way that they click a "print" button. Where that production takes place may follow a similar trend as printing: first in established regions with the cluster of pulping, printing, binding plants; later in print-on-demand service providers with strong transport capabilities; and finally in something like the Espresso Machine (http://ondemandbooks. com/) a device about the size of a kitchen table which can be located anywhere and prints books from a large online catalog in minutes, including color or size variations.

For the skeptics among the readers it's important to realize both the extent to which this will change supply chains and also the speed at which it could reach critical adoption. A brief look at some items already being produced through 3D printing and distributed manufacturing shows that not much will be left with centralized, twentieth century manufacturing techniques. For example, companies like Modern Meadow are already demonstrating cultured 3D printed meat production. They can literally take data on the tissue of an animal from one area, such as the famed pastures of Kobe, Japan, and print a steak of the same tissue in another part of the world. This example should help people think outside the box about how far supply chains may be disrupted or redefined by distributed manufacturing and the maker movement. In the meat printing example, there is still a supply chain, it is just radically different in nature from the dead-animal-carcass model it replaces. To be specific, the total kilogram-kilometer value of the supply chain is greatly reduced, the lead times are likely greatly reduced, and the importance of information management are greatly increased.

And remember: this is a near-term technology trend. Distributed manufacturing may seem like an "atoms not bits" business because it's about building "things." But a closer inspection may prove otherwise. The raw inputs to distributed manufacturing are abundant commodities like metals, plastics, and silicon. The transformational steps done to the raw materials require machinery, of course, but how those machines get the job done is a matter of design, and it is the design of the machines that is going to benefit from the exponential increase in computing, which connects the pace of distributed manufacturing back to the pace of computing. The improvements in design of all manner of machines or devices follows a curve tied to our ability to information process. And each improvement in *design* can introduce orders of magnitude of improvement to the *material* process. As a quick example, the production of a cup of tea could use five kilograms of wood if done on a poorly made open fire, or just a small amount of electricity if done through a high efficiency kettle.

To use a fun example, the invention of the wheel happened about 3500 BCE and yet it took until 1970 for luggage to have wheels added to it, and really another 10 to 15 years before stable designs emerged (i.e. the two wheels with a retractable handle coming up to natural hand height and keeping the bag at about 45 degrees during movement). The appearance of wheeled luggage had an instant impact on the porter industry, because it enabled most people to be able to handle their own bags while traveling whereas previously this was not true. The point here is that breakthroughs in design (a question of "bits") can suddenly reduce the direct material requirements (a question of "atoms") to produce the same results. It's reasonable to expect that design improvement on the methods of distributed manufacturing will be rapid and reinforcing (since they already have been), leading to a fast rollout into diverse supply chains.

Redefining the Optimal Quantity

Supply chain analysts spend a great deal of time trying to identify optimal quantities to produce at given sites, in given time frames, and with given configurations. Most of the attention around optimal quantity is in the supply-side of the equation, specifically in trying to achieve economies of scale and dealing with non-linearity in the costs or time-cycles of direct or indirect supply activities. These are complex planning tasks that require a fair amount of specialized tools and optimization software. The maker movement and distributing manufacturing often tout that they represent a shift towards economies of demand: in other words, single-unit production. This may be an oversimplification, extrapolating from prototyping or hobbyist activity to how true demand might be serviced. But the underlying statement is sound: distributed manufacturing is geared towards flexible fulfillment of demand in such a way that there is very little economy of scales to be achieved by higher volume production. Not that this necessarily simplifies the supply chain. On the contrary, any simplification of the optimal batch size is overshadowed by the fact that many, many new potential points of production would be added to the network. Allocating production and coordinating between them will be a significant challenge for supply chain practitioners.

Redefining the Time to Market

Distributed manufacturing and the maker movement herald great changes in the average time to market for products moving through supply chains. Even for products that remain difficult to manufacture outside concentrated sites, the rapid and distributed prototyping capabilities in the maker movement are already at work. For example, in the furniture industry full-scale prototypes can be printed on 3D printers overnight so that the design team and the sourcing team can discuss via teleconference the specification changes. This is already happening in areas like furniture, jewelry and accessories, mechanical parts, and medical devices. One of the most interesting areas in which distributed manufacturing has greatly reduced prototyping time is in biomedical products, because very recently labs have opened at key points around the world which can take (very large) data files containing genomic data, sequence samples of the biological materials, and ship them to the customer. This has been done with viruses, bacteria, and various tissues of human or animal origin.

In his Long Now Foundation presentation, former *Wired* magazine editor Chris Anderson compared the incredible speed available from distributed manufacturing to the process most products go through on their way to market (Anderson, 2013). To paraphrase, a typical IT hardware product like a GPS enabled watch for tracking a runner's workout will involve a sourcing trip to China or Taiwan. The sourcing agent will hire a translator, drive out to various factories, and begin a day-long or multi-day long inspection. The factory owner and the sourcing agent drink some green tea, view the operation, and try to establish capabilities and capacity. After a dinner meeting and some karaoke, the initial specifications may be shared. Then weeks or months pass as various pre-production prototypes are produced and sent to third parties for testing. Finally, a large batch order is sent and the buyer's funds locked into a letter of credit. From apparel to airplanes, this is a typical supply chain as it ramps up on new SKUs heading to market. The process is slow, capital intensive, and very exposed to the risks of changing demand. While distributed manufacturing offers the low hanging fruit of reduced direct transportation time, itself a modest gain in time to market, its more substantial offering is the ability to prototype without the need to negotiate access to specialized production capabilities. Each step in the current sourcing and product development process acts as an intentional or unintentional gate of the creative individual, team, or enterprise as it tries to meet current market demand. By reducing those steps, whole new classes of products will reach market and do so while demand is still close to what was seen during the design phase. Although this will certainly be used in consumer-entertainment products, it has much broader implications.

Here is an example of how distributed manufacturing has the potential to reshape supply chain time to market considerably. The current approach to immunizing a susceptible population against influenza is to look at data about various strands from a broad sample set and extrapolate outwards as much as 12 months. That much extrapolation is needed to produce large quantities of the vaccines and distribute them to the various regions that will need them. In the USA, the center for disease control commits to a vaccine profile by the end of the year so that manufacturing begins in January for inoculations occurring in September or October. Such a long time between production and usage allows for antigenic drift or the arrival of a new strain which will not be affected by the immunization. In the past 22 years, the US center for disease control reports that the strain selection failed considerably for four of those years. Unsurprisingly, distributed manufacturing is being applied to this problem. Already there is exchange of prototyping data for the inoculation formulation, so that facilities can produce small batches for testing. But one goal of the US center for disease control is to achieve very short lead-time production across the USA so that the sampling of local, rather than national, influenza viruses can be used to inoculate the population in as little as a week. The idea is that local pharmacies or doctors' offices will get daily data recipes in the same way our computers get updates pushed to them to close security flaws as they are discovered. They can then "print" their vaccines in the office or at a site in their city, and give their patients shots with a much higher chance of statistically relevant protection.

Bringing it Together: How the Maker Movement Impacts Supply Chain Visibility

The maker movement, like the personal computer culture of the 1970s and 1980s, has the potential to introduce enormously disruptive technologies into current supply chains. As the trailing edge of distributed manufacturing creeps forward it will open entirely new capabilities for bringing products to market.

A supply chain manager (and their counterparts in competitor organizations) will be faced with producing in new geographies, in much smaller but more frequent batches, and with faster introductions of revised or new products. The increased speed, batch size flexibility, and geographic assignment will simply multiply the supply chain coordination complexity. This is where visibility comes in to the picture, since the supply chain visibility meta use-case is in supporting more precise and nuanced coordination strategies. It's also worth noting that the maker movement is heading towards smaller individual companies or manufacturing sites. In other words, if this trend continues the standard will be for distributed manufacturing at sites which are not directly owned or controlled by the company producing through them. That is a classic supply chain cross-organization coordination challenge, one that supply chain visibility will need to support.

How much impact would the rise of distributed manufacturing have on supply chain visibility processes currently in use? Probably quite a large impact. Start by considering the emergence of many new sites of production and the re-design of the supply chain geography at a fundamental level. This will introduce a large number of sites which need to be made visible to centralized or distributed planning. As an analogy, consider the challenge that retailers face when making their points of sale transparent in terms of capacity and inventory. Typically those points of sale are being supported by a small number of points of production, but what if there were an equal number of production sites as points of sale, and those production sites were not even under the direct control of the retailer? This is probably challenging on a whole new order of magnitude compared to the requirements on current visibility solutions. Secondly, the distributed manufacturing paradigm would not only be diverse geographically, but also faster to cycle from design to sale. That allows less time to detect signals through the visibility process and bring them to the decision makers. Any visibility process which relies on long cycle times (such as evaluating plan-actual-forecast on a weekly basis) would need to be rebuilt so as to support the faster overall product lifecycle. Together, faster cycles of more sites running smaller or non-standard batch sizes would be enough to force complete rethinking of visibility solutions currently in use.

The Internet of Things

The Internet of Things concept was first promulgated in 1999 by Kevin Ashton of MIT's AutoID center (the creators of the RFID standard, among other things), who pointed out that the internet's wealth of data and accessibility was in fact totally dependent on human efforts to get data into the internet and to retrieve it for some productive use. By using the term "Internet of Things" he cleverly points us to the inverse of the phrase, the fact that our current internet is an "Internet of People." He explained the concept as such:

> Today computers—and, therefore, the Internet—are almost wholly dependent on human beings for information. Nearly all of the roughly 50 petabytes (a petabyte is 1,024 terabytes) of data available on the Internet were first captured and created by human beings—by typing, pressing a record button, taking a digital picture or scanning a bar code. Conventional diagrams of the Internet include servers and routers and so on, but they leave out the most numerous and important routers of all: people (Ashton, 2009).

In the same sense, the predominance of data on the internet is implicitly for human consumption. What the Internet of Things movement is indicating is that this implicit orientation of the internet towards human data capture and human consumption is in the process of being eroded. Their expectation is that a set of enabling technologies will become widespread enough that the center of mass in data creation and consumption moves from human to "thing," where "thing" is a physical or virtual object.

There is an interesting parallel to be made between the rise of thing-to-thing data exchange and the historic shift in telecommunications. When the fiber optic trunk lines which make up the backbone of the global internet were first laid down in the 1980s and 1990s, they were intended primarily for telephone communication. Building and maintaining that network was a truly global undertaking and it was implicitly to support "people talking to people." The same should be said about the later inclusion of microwave radio towers for mobile phones. But within 20 years, the center of gravity in usage had shifted dramatically. Today it is estimated that 1 percent of the telecommunication network capacity is used for voice communication, such a low portion that in many modes it's given away for free as part of the more important data traffic going into and out of personal electronics. What the Internet of Things movement suggests is that a similar shift is underway which will lead to an overwhelming portion of the internet being devoted to communication between non-human objects.

The Internet of Things specifically focuses on the supply chain as an initial driver in its technology roadmap. It's no coincidence that the term was coined by the person who also led the RFID standards creation, and a former Proctor

& Gamble supply chain manager. At its base, the movement suggests that the stuff being moved through the supply chain will convert from a passive to an active role in that process. The products, or the material handling units which contain them, will start executing tasks which are done today by humans on their behalf. They will count themselves as they move through facilities, check their own expiration dates or shelf life, notify their owners if a recall is being made on their production lot, assign their serial number to a customer's records, and validate their demand at a forecasted destination before being transported. If this sounds unreasonable, consider that all of these tasks are in fact being done today on behalf of the products by either software or humans. It's not so unreasonable to assume that the locus of action can shift down to the products directly.

In the supply chain context, the Internet of Things is growing based on three specific developments. Firstly, the ability to uniquely identify smaller and smaller physical things. For example, this is seen in the supply chain management trend towards unique identification of every pallet, then each case, and finally each individual product (such as with serial numbers). The MIT AutoID center referred to this trend as the growth in "unique addressability of things." Secondly, the growing sensorium given to data capturing devices, and the growth in the absolute number of these devices. Thirdly, the advancement of decentralized coordination technologies. This last factor is the least mature, but is being advanced in academic and industrial research settings. In one mode of this technology self-organizing peer-to-peer networks based on Bluetooth technology already exist. For example, imagine ten people in a room with smartphones and nine of them have just lost internet connections. Through a self-organizing Bluetooth-based network the smartphone users can still exchange information or even leverage the working phone's internet connection. Industrial scale examples of this in supply chain contexts are not easy to find, but the research points to a future where companies move away from centralized systems for running their businesses towards a collection of individual systems which are able to negotiate independently (and reliably) towards dynamic working relationships. The best metaphor for this is that the software would adapt to a new software component in the same way people adapt to a new colleague in their team: first they train and monitor, then they afford enough trust for the new team member to make decisions, and finally the total productivity rises based on the better division of labor around each person's specialization. In the same way, these systems would be self-healing when software components go offline, just as a team of people can get by when a colleague is out of the office.

HOW THE INTERNET OF THINGS IMPACTS SUPPLY CHAIN VISIBILITY

From a supply chain visibility perspective, the Internet of Things has a lot of potential for the way supply chains are managed. The most important change it has to offer is a paradigm of nearly ubiquitous identification and sensory data. This goes right to the heart of supply chain visibility's first step of data collection. In the current approach of most supply chain visibility processes, data capture is done by people. They are counting the boxes, checking for damage, scanning the barcodes, keying in arrival dates, and so forth. Even following the "key once, share often" strategy (which is best practice for many modes of data acquisition) implies that a human is doing the initial "key once" action to capture the data. The Internet of Things movement is making technologies which partially or totally subsume that process into the products themselves. This is not the same as automation alone, because automating the current visibility process would simply replace the human capture but would not move the locus of responsibility from the supply chain management staff to the product being managed. In the context of increased use of facilities or services which are not owned by the supply chain coordinator organization, this is an important distinction. Self-identifying or self-sensing products should be more adaptable to new channels of supply flow, such as a new facility or destination. But it would still be a significant challenge to redesign the visibility solutions as they exist today so that they are capable of interfacing with self-identifying and self-sensing products.

The second impact the Internet of Things movement should have on supply chain visibility is the trend towards non-human consumers of the visibility data. Most of the impact on supply chain decisions that visibility solutions have today is to influence or interrupt human decision makers. It isn't always like this (think about automated inventory allocation decisions which rely on supply chain visibility to know the state of inventory in upstream locations). But advances in the Internet of Things technology roadmap would lead to more and more non-human consumers of the visibility data, sometimes the products being moved but other times as third party objects which are positioned at some decision-making point in the supply chain. Gearing the visibility output to be useful to those objects will require redesigning several aspects, from the time latency between events to the data format and delivery mechanics.

Both of the expected impacts described above should increase the scale and complexity of the visibility solution. For example, a relatively simple shift from tracking each pallet to tracking each individual product is already something that overloads many visibility solutions. There is a related phenomenon already observed that increases in data capture technology like RFID tend to produce a lot of non-value-adding data because the systems are broadcasting or collecting data even if a relevant business event has not taken place. In terms of complexity, if there is overlap or expected interdependence on the data collected between the things in the supply chain this opens many new data relationships which would have to be managed. For example, if products begin to self-identify, but only some other object like a pallet or carnet has the required sensorium to detect GPS coordinates, there must be a managed relationship between the sensory data and the product ID. Aspects such as these will likely challenge supply chain visibility systems in early adopter companies until best practices are established.

Human-Machine Symbiosis

The concept behind human-machine symbiosis dates back as far as the 1960s (Licklider, 1960). Conceptually it repositions the division of work and role of computers compared to the human users. Rather than orienting computers to automate and therefore replace human staff, the focus is on augmenting the capabilities of the human user. Artificial intelligence research, such as that done by Hans Moravec and Marvin Minsky in the 1980s, show that there may be a fruitful division of task or task components between human and machine because machines tends to excel at deep deductive logic or mathematical-based tasks while being challenged to match the skills of a child when it comes to perception and mobility. This is the Moravec Paradox. When successful, human-machine symbiosis results in human participation in problem solving or task execution where natural human capabilities would be a limiting factor. Wholly different and often times better results can be achieved by complimenting rather than replacing the human user.

Given that the term originated over 50 years ago, it may be hard to see why it is being included in the list of technologies which have the potential to radically change supply chain visibility. In fact, human-machine symbioses is just coming into its maturity. Sub-fields such as software usability engineering are still relatively young. Perhaps a good indicator of the change in zeitgeist is from the field of human-machine chess tournaments. Almost as soon as computation was being done mechanically there was an interest in pitting computers against human players in a confrontational role. This went on for a long time, with serious academic attention being done for at least 50 years. Ultimately the purpose-built, extremely powerful IBM machine Deep Blue achieved a victory over reigning world champion Garry Kasparov in 1997. The fact that IBM's machine was victorious was seen as a kind of heralding of a new time. So called "Narrow Artificial Intelligence" was appearing in diverse activities that had once been "human only." This was understandably frightening to those who faced computer competition. Garry Kasparov himself seemed to take his defeat hard. But what happened since then is important to understand how the technology focus is shifting.

Since the Deep Blue victory of 1997, the research interest in computer chess turned to collaborative approaches where the human and machine work together, as a team, against an opponent who is also a team comprised of a computer and a human. This style of chess is called "advanced chess" and has been promoted by none other than former world champion Garry Kasparov. Firstly, it's interesting to note that between 1997 and today, computers never completely dominated human players in chess. The top 200 players have maintained an average win rate of about 45 percent, and the top 20 worldwide chess masters maintain even ranking with the computer opponents. Even in a well-defined optimization space like chess, human ingenuity has its value. We should expect it to hold even more so in the supply chain field where rules of engagement are large, complex, and open to being challenged. To close the chess analogy, consider why advanced chess has emerged with such a passionate following. To paraphrase the words of Garry Kasparov, it delivers consistently great games by combining strategic style (mostly from the human) with rigorous exploration of the available options tree (mostly by the computer). Tactical exploitation of an opponent's errors is almost guaranteed, but also the chance of those kinds of errors being made is greatly reduced. Now imagine what that kind of augmented tactical and strategic thinking could look like when applied to supply chains of competitive companies. It's an exciting possibility.

HOW HUMAN-MACHINE SYMBIOSIS IMPACTS SUPPLY CHAIN VISIBILITY

Human-machine symbiosis in supply chain visibility is largely targeted at the way intelligence is integrated into decision making, the last step in the visibility process. In the last five years, all the major software vendors who provide visibility solutions have made focused efforts to improve their touch points with the human users. This is a first step, but hardly revolutionary. What may be coming in the near future is a tidal wave of new user interaction styles driven by a redirection of Silicon Valley energies from consumer software to enterprise software. Consumer applications (notably the Apple products) have already embraced the fact that every user interaction faces potential friction from a less than perfect software interface. Unlike in the enterprise space, where users are employees who have to use the software they are told to use, consumer applications can lose market share or even their entire company if the friction is too high. This divide in how the user's experience is treated has led to a substantial gulf between the usability of consumer vs. enterprise software applications. At some point, either the tricks of consumer applications will be integrated by enterprise software vendors, or consumer software vendors will migrate towards enterprise categories. There has been plenty of time for enterprise software vendors to adapt already, so it's more likely that the fast-growing and experienced consumer-software vendors will be driving this change.

How would this specifically affect visibility? Firstly, it should make visibility much more impactful and valuable to the businesses that use it. The user experience acts as a silent gating criterion on how much of the decision process will be influenced by the visibility intelligence. If the process of getting that visibility intelligence is slow and painful for the user, they will be less likely to use it. When Human-Machine Symbiosis technologies culminate in truly enjoyable interactions with the visibility system, the gating effect is reduced. Secondly, improved user experiences would likely lead to more visibility overall, because one part of a satisfying experience is consistent and constant access. Users can't be intimately tied in with multiple visibility solutions or a single solution which has byzantine quality or behavior based on what sub-system is feeding it. This will be a heavy burden on the creation and operation of supply chain visibility solutions because they will need to be much more consistent than they are today. Lastly, it's reasonable to assume that visibility as a perk from logistics service providers will face much more scrutiny than today when it comes to usability. This is something which is seen as secondary today (see discussion above about enterprise software's view on user interaction).

Machine Learning

Machine learning is part of the more general and ambiguous area of artificial intelligence (AI). But unlike AI, machine learning largely avoids the ethical and philosophical issues which appear when the resulting application is targeting self-awareness or autonomy of action. Instead, machine learning as a field focuses on creating adaptive technologies which learn from patterns in the data which they consume, and which produce differing outputs as a result. Machine learning has made important advances in the last ten years, not just in basic research but in applied and broadly deployed use cases as well. Unfortunately, as with its parent topic of AI, any time a critical learning barrier is broken it somehow is transformed instantly from "intelligence" to "computation." Here is an example: one sub-area of machine learning is machine vision, such as identifying a person's unique face among a crowd. This is an area that has seen total revolution in the last ten years. A user of a social networking site like Google+ or Facebook can upload their digital photographs and the software will pick out the faces from the photos and give a suggestion on the name of the person from among the user's social group. The software learns from its mistakes, because every suggestion has to be validated by the user and this reinforces good selections while learning from bad selections. It's likely that within the next ten years a very large percentage of all photos of people on the internet will have automated identification applied to them as a background process. Before this technology became widespread, the ability to recognize an individual by their face in a variety of angles, lighting, clothes, haircuts, facial affects, and so forth, would be considered human-only level of intelligence. Now it's just computation.

Machine learning is not just interesting: it is vital to the success of other technology adoptions which would increase the rate of data acquisition (see the topic further down on "Big Data"). Without support from adaptive software which can execute greater and greater pre-processing tasks, the flood of data would overwhelm us. Machine learning technology acts like power steering on vehicles; a support mechanism which is almost invisible when implemented correctly but greatly magnifies the performance of the system. It's this aspect that is the most germane for the field of supply chain visibility. As machine learning advances it will act as a foundation upon which the true user interaction is built, focusing business analysts and supply chain management onto only those tasks too subtle, ambiguous, or strategic to be learned by the software itself. This is analogous to the way that auto-complete of words enables a smartphone user to focus on their email or text message content. The auto-complete features on smartphones are in fact machine learning applications, which start with a broad dictionary and then adapt to the much smaller lexicon favored by the user. We can expect to see similar applications in supply chain visibility where the user's revealed behavior gets incorporated into the supply chain visibility software in order to greatly reduce user friction.

Three sub-fields of machine learning have particular importance for the future of supply chain visibility solutions: natural language processing, machine perception, and recommender systems. Natural language processing refers to the ability for human language (such as an email in English) to be directly consumed by a machine and for the same sense-making to be achieved compared to a human recipient. As this area progresses our preferred models for human-machine interaction are likely to shift dramatically towards the same approach we use with other people. For example, when a transport analysts wants to get a summary of late deliveries from a visibility solution today, they have to go to an application, navigate to a page, enter structured data in a specific sequence, and then re-format the output data to match their needs. But if the same analyst has to ask a co-worker to do the task, they do so through an email with a short paragraph of English text. When the co-worker needs clarification, they just ask. This model of interaction, which focuses on dialogue, is more intuitive for people and it's exactly what can happen as natural language processing becomes more robust. In a supply chain visibility solution, natural language processing would probably figure prominently as part of the data integration process and also the interruption of decision making (by giving decision makers a natural language synopsis instead of data tables, for example). Recent start-ups such as Narrative Science are already doing this in similar business fields, such as marketing or retail operations. Their software consumes large data sets and then produces a summary in natural language. As an example, the business journal *Forbes* is using this software to produce articles based on structured earnings reports from publicly listed companies, previously a job for high-skilled analysts and journalists. Here is an example taken from the *Forbes* website:

> *Analysts expect decreased profit for* Nabors Industries (NBR) *when the company reports its first quarter results on Tuesday, April 23, 2013. Although Nabors reported profit of 49 cents a year ago, the consensus estimate calls for earnings per share of 29 cents.*

> *The consensus estimate has fallen over the past three months, from 35 cents. For the fiscal year, analysts are expecting earnings of $1.18 per share. Analysts project revenue to fall 10.4% year-over-year to $1.65 billion for the quarter, after being $1.84 billion a year ago. For the year, revenue is expected to come in at $6.57 billion.*

> *A decline in revenue in the fourth quarter of the last fiscal year snapped a streak of three consecutive quarters of growing revenue. Revenue fell 4.5% in the fourth quarter of the last fiscal year and rose 0.9% in the third quarter of the last fiscal year, 18% in the second quarter of the last fiscal year and 30.7% in the first quarter of the last fiscal year.*

Most analysts think investors should stand pat on Nabors, with 11 of
19 analysts rating it hold. Analysts have become more optimistic about
the stock recently and the number of buy ratings has risen slightly over
the past three months.[1]

Reading the text above must give supply chain managers a moment of reflection. If a piece of software can write that report within a second of the data being published, what could such a natural language processing technology do in their company? This is directly relevant to supply chain visibility because the last two process steps for any visibility solution are the creation of intelligence based on the data, and the interruption of decisions with that intelligence. Currently a lot of executive summary memos, PowerPoint decks, and daily dashboard reports are bubbling up from the raw data of visibility solutions in an attempt to hit a decision maker in the right format and the right time to guide them towards better decisions. Natural language processing offers a more intuitive method of getting those points across, and often in less time and with less cost.

The second sub-field of machine learning which has important implications for supply chain management and supply chain visibility is machine perception. Machine perception refers to the ability of machines to take in data from a variety of formats (optical, audio, and so forth) and to interpret the data in a way similar to human perception. It allows, for example, a computer to identify a traffic light from a dashboard video camera and correctly interpret what the object means in relation to the car's route (i.e. is it applicable to the car or is it facing another street). Machine perception has some great use cases in supply chains, perhaps the most important one being autonomous vehicles. The technical challenge of autonomous vehicles is mostly in the area of perception, since the data capture is fairly easy, the robotic control of the vehicle is simple, and the traffic rules can be compiled into logical guidelines. For supply chain visibility, machine perception could drastically change the way raw data is captured at supply chain sites. Although there is great potential in advances such as the Internet of Things in the domain of data capture, the truth is that many qualities of the physical supply chain need external perception to be evaluated. If the physical infrastructure sites in the supply chain had instruments embedded and that flow of data could be processed by a machine rather than people, the potential coverage of data capture for visibility would be greatly increased.

---

1   See http://www.forbes.com/sites/narrativescience/2013/04/19/forbes-earnings-preview-nabors
    -industries-6/

The third area of potential impact for supply chain visibility from machine learning is in the emergence of extraordinarily strong recommender systems. Anyone who conducts some shopping online would be familiar with the consumer applications of recommender systems. Amazon, eBay, Netflix, or nearly any other website with any social component deploy software to identify and recommend products or services which have a higher chance of being purchased by the shopper. Recommender systems do as their name implies: they recommend actions to the users by learning about their preferences, evaluating possible actions, and past outcomes from similar situations. Recommender systems appear in many of the tools we already use in supply chain contexts. But as their quality and pervasiveness increase, they may induce a true pivot in expectations about what defines an acceptable supply chain visibility solution. Recommender systems invert the onus of action from the user to the system by expecting the system to evaluate all options and reduce the scope of available options to only those which the user should be expected to consider in depth. In situations where there are orders of magnitude more choices that the user could possibly evaluate (such as selecting books from a book store) a smart and personalized filter on the selection process is crucial to usability. As the scope of visibility solutions grows to include more data and more decision interruption points, it makes sense that business users will expect greater recommendation filter tools to support them. In some ways this is already happening with the pressure to have good "dashboarding" in visibility systems. In effect, there is so much data in current visibility solutions that users are already demanding a filter which at least raises the critical items to the landing page dashboard. As machine learning improves, we can expect that tools like book recommending algorithms get adapted and applied to visibility systems such that what is "important" is no longer a configured pattern decided during system design, but a pattern which emerges from the user's (or their peer's) direct behavior with the system.

Big Data

The overall volume of data being captured is growing exponentially over time. As a small example, Google published a white paper in late 2008 showing the processed roughly 20 petabytes of data per day. Not only is data *volume* growing, but the data is rapidly expanding along several other dimensions such as:

1. Variety: more kinds of data being captured, particularly true of unstructured or complex structured data such as free text or voice or video.

2.   Frequency: the number of times an object will have its data captured during its lifecycle.

3.   Breadth: a single record or object tends to contain more information.

4.   Distribution: the same record or related records are stored in multiple environments and must be coordinated during update or retrieval.

Strictly speaking, the field of "Big Data" is defined as the problem of dealing with data sets which are so large as to be impossible to curate or use. But this definition has drawbacks, namely that what is "overwhelmingly large" in terms of data management is different depending on the company and the specific task being undertaken. Search providers like Google are managing double digit petabytes of data on a daily basis; the US library of congress is managing at least two orders of magnitude less (they claim to have collected about 250 terabytes in total). Logistics service providers such as parcel carriers or freight forwarders are typically actively managing one or less terabyte per day, a full two orders of magnitude below the library of congress. Finally, small and medium-sized enterprises may have much less than one terabyte in total in their core supply chain visibility systems. What this means is that the impacts of big data will not appear to all supply chains at the same time.

Common usage of the term "big data" also stands in for the more general wave of huge data volumes even if they can be managed by the data owner. Therefore it is also sometimes called "ubiquitous data." This is the context for most supply chain managers who are dealing with big data, because they are in a grey zone where they are deeply challenged but still able to cope with the data. But they can see the trend and understand that data acquisition is occurring faster than integration or sense-making advances are being deployed. One component of big data which is particularly challenging is the fact that the data is often distributed across heterogeneous systems, such that distributed data management must be used because there is not a single normalized set of tables to query against. On a more technical level, the distributed quality of big data stresses the very core of visibility technologies because it challenges the two fundamental drivers of modern databases: the need to abstract the structure of data and the need to efficiently manipulate the data (Bierman, Buneman, and Gardner, 2003). Relational databases achieved their dominance as the backbone for visibility systems due to their ability to simplify (i.e. abstract) data in a tabular format and provided a fast way to perform algebraic operations on the structured data (Bierman, Buneman, and Gardner, 2003). But both of these features are stressed or completely fail in the presence of widely distributed data, particularly when no one system has total control over the data. As one would expect, this is very germane to the topic of supply chain visibility where the current and future needs will involve coordinating many separate and autonomous systems as they exchange data in real time. One likely consequence of the onslaught of big data will be a shift to database paradigms that support distributed data storage and greater scale, such as no-SQL or Hadoop approaches. These may not provide ACID processing, but in many situations eventual consistency is acceptable.

So it's fair to say that Big Data has the potential to stress supply chain visibility systems. But it has other potential as well. The presence of so much data obviously signals the opportunity to know more about our supply chains. For organizations who can handle it, the deluge of data will open doors for faster, more accurate, and more pervasive use of visibility to optimize supply chains. The nature of Big Data may result in more focus given to data usage rather than data capture, as is often the case for supply chain visibility systems, since the current blind spots or sensorium gaps will be likely closed.

9

Conclusion

Supply chain visibility started out as an ambiguous synonym for the quality or quantity of information access or sharing in the supply chain. Typical usages of the term in the 1980s or early 1990s were along the lines of "that company has a high degree of visibility to their upstream inventory." By the late 1990s a new definition was taking hold, one that assumed that supply chain visibility was a solution rather than a quality to be measured. Publications and conference presentations leveraged the new definition in phrases like "an important addition to your supply chain visibility." Although the term's meaning hasn't shifted as profoundly since the late 1990s, it remained ambiguous and variously defined by later researchers or practitioners.

Regardless of the definitional framework, research into supply chain visibility produced several theoretical constructs of importance. Among these are the facts that organizational willingness and data quality are key determinants of successful supply chain visibility projects. The work on how technology influences visibility showed that visibility was enabled but not outright dominated by technology decisions, similar to most business processes in the supply chain. And a number of studies in different years demonstrated important correlations between the presence of supply chain visibility and positive overall business outcomes.

The weaknesses in the past research agenda included a poor definitional framework for the subject, a lack of clear prerequisites which must be present for visibility to work, and most importantly a methodology for assessing the visibility effectiveness or efficiency, particularly with the purpose of comparing multiple visibility solutions against each other. This book proposed a novel framework covering these three points, which readers or later researchers can adapt and improve on as they experiment with them.

In practical settings, the supply chain management community has seen wide variations in how visibility solutions are designed and deployed. The book reviewed eight popular types of visibility, including why those models might be considered a good fit for a given situation. Although not an exhaustive list, the eight types of visibility reviewed provide a broad range of meta-patterns which can be repurposed to understanding or building many more types of visibility solutions.

Because the practitioner community often is challenged with the technology acquisition process around visibility, the book covered this in great detail. Supply chain managers have effectively four options: Buy, Rent, Build, or Borrow. The options were first compared and then reviewed separately in more detail. Since the area with the least available resources is the option to build in-house solutions, this was given good depth with the inclusion of design patterns for the data object relationships behind different visibility solution types. In the chapter on visibility technology vendors the top three software providers (a mix of license, single tenant SaaS, and multi-tenant SaaS) were reviewed and contrasted.

Finally, critical technology trends were discussed along with their potential impacts on the domain of supply chain visibility. These trends are all past the proof of concept phase and entering ramp-up towards broad usage. How that ramp-up plays out will greatly determine what is considered an acceptable visibility solution by the end of the decade.

The field of supply chain visibility is a niche in a niche, a place for extreme specialization. But it is nonetheless important and impactful. When visibility solutions are being proposed, designed, evaluated, implemented, or operated in a business the supply chain managers need to understand the underlying principles and the scope of what should and could achieve the best results. Hopefully this book has met the needs of professionals in this space who are becoming involved in supply chain visibility and engaged in their careers enough to sit down and study the topic. For those interested, Appendix A includes transcripts of several practitioner interviews and Appendix B includes a sample supply chain visibility scorecard instrument.

Appendix A

Transcripts from Interviews with Practitioners

Lienhard, Christoph (Vice President of Supply Chain Business Consulting at Panalpina). 2013. Supply Chain Visibility. Interviewed by Jonah McIntire [in person with subsequent text review] Basel, CH on 15 February 2013. Transcript follows:

1.   [Question from Jonah McIntire]   How does your company come to the supply chain visibility topic? What major work are you doing or have done in this field?

[Response from Christoph Lienhard]   It's really two sides, two activities. The first is that it is a fundamental of our business to deliver our services at the expected quality. We are an international business, not just a multi-national. Our business is always across countries. It's like we have a factory and the four walls are the edges of the globe. We should know everything in that factory. But to know the status of all activities is a challenge, especially when running asset light. In production environments, you can always go out and physically see the activity. But in an asset-light context, you are not only spaced out geographically but also in terms of processes with subcontractors. Also our customers expect absolute transparency. Panalpina is expected to handle the physical freight, but also to handle data from multiple parties, such as order and SKU data. Our customers expect us to operate like a glass-house, to see from top to bottom and from source to destination their entire flow. We ultimately do not manage supply chains, but enable others to manage their supply chains. We are not engaged with point of sales, with forecasting, etc., so we're an input for another party who is the true supply chain manager.

2.   [Question from Jonah McIntire]   You step into an elevator with the new CEO of your company, and she asks you what supply chain visibility is about. How do you define it before the elevator doors open?

       [Response from Christoph Lienhard]   The simple answer would be that it provides all stakeholders in the supply chain with relevant information. Relevant means that such information is a mandatory input for the product or actions. Visibility is about information, but information has to be relevant. A lot of this is transactional, such as track and trace. But not necessarily everything. Providing such information, either we push or we provide tools for people to pull as needed. In summary, relevancy of information is critical.

3.   [Question from Jonah McIntire]   What gets mixed up into the supply chain visibility which you feel should be left out? How do practitioners sharpen the blurry lines on the subject?

       [Response from Christoph Lienhard]   It's often a buzz word, and at the end it depends on the individual, the role, the function, and the business need. As an example, the person sitting in front of a warehouse dock door needs to have visibility about deliveries for today. On the other end, the global supply chain manager needs visibility but an entire different kind. So sometimes visibility needs the context of the target user or use case in order to be properly defined. For example, reporting (business intelligence) is not visibility, but in some situations visibility uses those tools.

4.   [Question from Jonah McIntire]   Are there fundamentally different kinds of visibility or just different implementation approaches to achieving the same goal?

       [Response from Christoph Lienhard]   In the end we're talking about 100 percent transparency on everything that happened (to see the past and make better decisions on the future), and then forecasted events for the future, and then at different levels of aggregation. So we're talking about the same topic with no subsets (visibility), but with different scopes (granularity, time lines, scope of information) it can appear to be different kinds of visibility.

5.   [Question from Jonah McIntire]   How did you first get involved with supply chain visibility (either as an individual or a company)?

[Response from Christoph Lienhard] In the strictest sense it would be in 1989 when I was starting a trucking company in Mali. I would go find trucks by literally driving around the major roads of the city to find my fleet parked in front of someone's house. No phones, no GPS, no checkpoints for 500 kilometers, so this was a real mess. We talk about SKU level visibility today but there are places in this world where you can lose a truck for weeks. I had a customer who talked about visibility to inventory cycle times for cell phones in Africa and especially their SIM cards. He expected visibility along the lines of European warehouses. But with the situation on the ground that was not realistic.

6.   [Question from Jonah McIntire] How would you suggest practitioners select the most appropriate method for themselves?

[Response from Christoph Lienhard] Let's make an assumption: in most industries traditional supply chain managers must treat the supply chain as core to the company's overall value-chain activities and within the supply chain activity visibility is mission-critical and key success factor. However, for the company *overall supply chain visibility* may be important, but it's neither mission-critical nor a competitive differentiator to succeed in the market place. Apple will not outsource their design, for example, because it is both mission-critical and competitive differentiating. Supply chain visibility is not in the same category. That being said, I suggest outsourcing. Especially because there are options available that may be faster, cheaper, and/or more specialized. Do not waste time trying to recreate connections to carriers, to suppliers, etc. But retain in-house the staff and tools to make use of the visibility which you get. So, outsource the production but retain management and decision-support. It's like in tier 1 or tier 2 manufacturer in automotive, who must focus their supplier management down to a smaller number of providers, who are then doing more sourcing on their behalf.

Now, in terms of SaaS vs. receiving visibility as a perk from a logistics company. Current SaaS options are like a gateway, basically a simpler way to get the data inputs for gathering data. Logistics providers are an aggregator, but also a real provider of services. So they can action the decisions coming from the visibility. In some situations it might be good to add a final additional layer to aggregate multiple logistics providers, and this may be a good use of SaaS options. In the end, it comes down to the cost-benefit proposition of each provider. Usually there is a risk and cost associated with adding a SaaS provider who is a middle-man between the buyer and the logistics service provider. This depends a lot on scale. With a smaller company we have to ask "what is the value of a middleman"? The middle-man will always be dependent on the principle parties, so it might be best to first try to get the services from the principles directly unless there is a higher benefit/cost ratio of adding an additional middle layer.

7.   [Question from Jonah McIntire] What kind of timelines do you consider normal for a successful visibility project? How far apart are milestones like project proposal, approval, kick-off, go-live, and pay-back?

      [Response from Christoph Lienhard] Starting from nothing, within six months you can have something decent that gives a lot of value and shows results and is workable. It's not a month but it's also not a year, so it's in-between. But this is a Pareto distribution because the last 20 percent are *hard*. They are almost a never ending story to keep covering the long tail of requirements.

8.   [Question from Jonah McIntire]   Is supply chain visibility fundamentally a technology topic?

      [Response from Christoph Lienhard] You need technology to do it properly, especially to consume and process the data. But to produce the data, perhaps it's a different story.

9.   [Question from Jonah McIntire]   Can you think of a technology change since 2000 which caused serious delay or advancement to supply chain visibility?

      [Response from Christoph Lienhard]   The internet penetration, because it is the platform for producing and also accessing supply chain visibility. To get the visibility inputs and then to provide them to the users, the internet is absolutely critical. Plus the entire market of software options, the number and capability of available tools, has grown tremendously.

10.   [Question from Jonah McIntire]   Supply chains are cross-organizational, but specific investments in technology, training, and coordination need to be made for supply chain visibility. Do you see examples of these things being shared among the supply chain partners, or are they typically owned and managed by one party?

[Response from Christoph Lienhard] Eventually everyone in the supply chain is paying for these costs, but the cost sharing comes out in the transactional pricing instead of one-off project budgets. Just like a computer adds no value when it's on a shelf and not used, there is a similar lack of value from just having "visibility." So we should distinguish between the setup costs and investments, but also the ongoing usage, the process redesign, etc. And those costs should be paid by the individual companies in the supply chain and they should have their own clear paybacks from these costs. In other words, there is a difference between the setup costs to build the visibility "product" from the operating costs for using that product.

For the operating costs, these have to bake into the transactional costs, such as the transport fees (for a transporter) or the per-piece price (for a manufacturer). The business community will no longer accept line-item costs for visibility, because it's just a minimum part of delivering normal business.

Wilkie, Graham (eCommerce Supply Chain Director at Carrefour). 2013. Supply Chain Visibility. Interviewed by Jonah McIntire [via telephone with subsequent text review] Basel, CH on 24 January 2013. Transcript follows:

1. [Question from Jonah McIntire]   How does your company come to the supply chain visibility topic? What major work are you doing or have done in this field?

    [Response from Graham Wilkie]   Carrefour has tried in the past, but the general theme of the company on systems is somewhat fragmented. Many of the stages in process are operated independently of each other. Logistics is well connected, but beyond logistics it becomes more fragmented.

2. [Question from Jonah McIntire]   You step into an elevator with the new CEO of your company, and she asks you what supply chain visibility is about. How do you define it before the elevator doors open?

    [Response from Graham Wilkie]   In my view, supply chain visibility is a fundamental activity of supply chain. It is not a differentiator but a requirement. In part I focus on (e-commerce), it is even more important.

When a customer selects a single SKU off a website they are expecting rapid and consistent delivery of that item. It is vital, a foundation.

3.   [Question from Jonah McIntire]   What gets mixed up into the supply chain visibility which you feel should be left out? How do practitioners sharpen the blurry lines on the subject?

[Response from Graham Wilkie] Supply chain visibility is a means, not an end. You must define what you are trying to achieve within the organization and how supply chain visibility can play a role. Where it really comes into its own is in medium to large organizations who are trying to achieve results in inventory turn, absolute inventory levels, cash flow, and availability.

4.   [Question from Jonah McIntire]   Are there fundamentally different kinds of visibility or just different implementation approaches to achieving the same goal?

[Response from Graham Wilkie]   I think the broad topic is the same, similar to the term "supply chain." If you put 20 people in a room and ask them to define supply chain you get a wide variety of answers. The same thing happens with the term "supply chain visibility."

The key question is "what will you do with this new information?" If you look at building supply chains from the consumer backwards, supply chain visibility is a tool for the fundamental question of "when can I have this product." This occurs after a customer has gone to the trouble of researching, going to the point of sale, and is often better informed (via mobile computing) than the sales staff. Supply chain visibility is needed to help close the gap between the sales staff and the customer. Supply chain visibility is also critical for things like "order online and collect in-store 2–4 hours later." This is especially true of products with high demand and low stock, because the customer has more incentive to reserve stock prior to visiting the store.

5.   [Question from Jonah McIntire]   What was the best or worst visibility initiative you've seen? Dialing back to the start of the project, what factors predicted the project outcome the most successfully?

[Response from Graham Wilkie]   When I was working with Kingfisher in the UK, the logistics activities were outsourced to Maersk as both a 3PL and 4PL. They initiated system development called "SPECTIVE," this is eight to ten years ago. What I saw was the most collaborative process I have encountered. Suppliers providing services trying to achieve true upstream visibility with their customers. They spent a long time trying to understand the customer's needs and then taking actions to meet them. The project was around two to two and a half years from beginning to end. The diversity of customer base and product base made this a challenging product. The missing element in this project was that it was trying to meet everyone's needs which prevented them from achieving critical mass. The lesson is that it's a difficult decision to make about when to customize the solution for a given client or product.

6.   [Question from Jonah McIntire]   Supply chain managers tend to acquire supply chain visibility through in-house development, off-the-shelf software, SaaS software, or as a perk from logistics service providers. How would you suggest practitioners select the most appropriate method for themselves?

      [Response from Graham Wilkie]   Inevitably every company is going to want a solution that is right for them. As an analogy, with a WMS you do not want to develop your own solution but acquire a licensed solution and then customize it to your needs. My preference, but it is a personal one, is to find best practices and future proofing from off-the-shelf solutions. The future proofing is important because when asked business practitioners (in the company) will focus on today's problems. But in several years they may change sourcing or operating specifications and end up with an over-fit solution to today's problems. This is particularly true of sourcing professionals who consider medium to long-term time horizons to less than 24 months. In recent business environments the chance of immediate and broad changes in the supplier base.

7.   [Question from Jonah McIntire]   Is supply chain visibility fundamentally a technology topic?

      [Response from Graham Wilkie]   No, it's first a strategy question, then a business process question, and third a technology question. In point of fact, you must define "what is the strategy for the supply chain and overall organization, right down to the relation (to the relation) to the customer."

You need sponsorship right from the top, right from the CEO. That's priority number one. Then the onus of the process is on supply chain leadership, as they understand the processes and implications. And secondarily the CIO, who understands the legacy systems and also how the infrastructure needs to be adapted.

But this is not always how it is done. I've seen it started by the supply chain organization, but without true sponsorship from the top. They are left with the challenge of engaging the CIO or IT group, who are matching this requirement with a million other requirements and with a budget which is constrained and cannot deliver the full requirements. The other issue is that the time frame for the project may be longer than the average tenure for the senior IT leadership, especially the CIO. This goes back to "boiling the ocean" where the breadth of work means it cannot be moved forward fast enough to be completed within the tenure period.

8.   [Question from Jonah McIntire]   What are some of the most critical technology trends which you see converging on supply chain visibility? Why will these be critical areas to watch?

[Response from Graham Wilkie]   I think topics like SaaS are becoming critical. On one hand you have massive ERP-style implementations which are long time frames and affect everyone, the result is a long project delivery but can be high quality. It always outlives the tenure of the originating leaders. With SaaS you have a series of small projects which serve the originators of the issues within the organization.

Business intelligence in itself is the ability to mine data out of non-integrated systems.

9.   [Question from Jonah McIntire]   An IBM Chief Supply Chain Officer survey came back with interesting results in 2009. It showed that 70 percent of Chief Supply Chain Officers considered supply chain visibility a top challenge, but not a top priority. The top reasons provided by the respondents were: organizational silos, the fact they were not rewarded for visibility improvements, and the lack of effective tools. It's been three years now, how do you feel about this outlook? Has it changed and in what ways?

[Response from Graham Wilkie]   Ironically, I think e-commerce is emerging as a field where the supply chain visibility must be answered with more rigor than in the past. As it grows in scale, it puts the supply chain visibility as a higher priority. Executives may see the issue of supply chain visibility as a parallel to environmental initiatives. There may be a near-universal agreement that this is important, but the perception is that very little impact can be done during their tenure. E-commerce may be changing this because it offers more potential for smaller-term and larger-impact supply chain visibility projects.

Karel, Peter (Senior Vice President and Global Head of Supply Chain Solutions at Panalpina). 2013. Supply Chain Visibility. Interviewed by Jonah McIntire [in person with subsequent text review] Basel, CH on 22 February 2013. Transcript follows:

1.   [Question from Jonah McIntire]   How does your company come to the supply chain visibility topic? What major work are you doing or have done in this field?

     [Response from Peter Karel]   What we provide is coming from our executional capabilities. Everything that is shipment related, i.e. transport focused. In addition, we do offer inventory visibility. And, we've implemented good business intelligence capabilities through SAP Information Explorer on HANA. Where we need to particularly focus on is in relation to our asset-right business model. We do not have our own network of vehicles and facilities. By not owning the distribution, and especially the last-mile or first-mile it is critical to carefully control the data capture or decision making. Generally, asset-right is a bigger challenge for visibility compared to an Integrator.

     Another area where we engage in and where visibility plays an important role is related to the planning or design side of supply chains. Mapping, analyzing and modeling different supply chain networks requires visibility on the physical network structure but also on the related material flows and product characteristics. We are using state-of-the-art software to support our customers in supply chain network design and optimization.

2.   [Question from Jonah McIntire]   You step into an elevator with the new CEO of your company, and she asks you what supply chain visibility is about. How do you define it before the elevator doors open?

[Response from Peter Karel]   Supply chain visibility is about knowing and controlling where products or materials are at within the business process. Looking at the SCOR process, for example, supply chain visibility tells us the state of those processes and the disposition of materials. As a metaphor, if you think about kids and you go on vacation by car for example, the father knows the geography, he has access to the map and the road conditions, he can use the radio or the phone to get additional updates, etc. The child is being transported and is constantly asking for the update on where they are at and what will happen next. This is similar to a supply chain visibility need because there is someone who has all the information, the bits and pieces needed to deduce the answer.

3.   [Question from Jonah McIntire]   What gets mixed up into supply chain visibility which you feel should be left out? How do practitioners sharpen the blurry lines on the subject?

[Response from Peter Karel]   I don't think there are too many things mixed up, but there are two distinct layers, both equally important. The first is a strategic level where we talk about the goals or targets of the company. The second is the operational visibility where we look at specific transactions and disposition of inventory or shipments. People tend to mix these too easily. We should try to separate them, focus on the strategic aspects first and then move to the transactional details.

4.   [Question from Jonah McIntire]   Are there fundamentally different kinds of visibility or just different implementation approaches to achieving the same goal?

[Response from Peter Karel]   From the terminology or definition, there is just one "supply chain visibility" in my opinion. But different industries will push to different levels of granularity. For example, in healthcare the granularity will be down into the batch or pedigree of specific devices or drugs. For oil and gas customers, they tend to be more focused on the tracking of oil well supplies or assets such as drill tools, without overt tracking on who originally built the tool, etc., although this might become relevant in certain situations as well of course (e.g. claims, rig-shut downs, etc.). The difference here is on the business need. It's about what is the impact of the visibility or the lack of visibility. If you take retail and fashion, with companies like Zara, the visibility or lack of it would drastically affect the dialing in of inventory to match actual demand.

There is also the important differentiation, even within an industry, of how each company tries to position itself against the competition. Cost-leaders will approach visibility completely differently from a fashion or service leader, for example.

5.   [Question from Jonah McIntire]   The management field is famous for fixating on topics and then discarding them a few years later. Do you think supply chain visibility is such a case? Is it a tool that is overhyped or undervalued?

     [Response from Peter Karel]   I don't believe it is overhyped. End-to-end supply chain visibility is in many cases still a challenge. On top, the functional/organizational importance of supply chain management and the respective impact on a company's performance has only during the last couple of years been recognized. Our recent 3PL Study reveals that the major frustration between Shippers and 3PLs lies in the lack of visibility. Hence, there is still a lot of improvement possible particularly if you think about the new technologies allowing mobile, anywhere access to data.

6.   [Question from Jonah McIntire]   What was the best or worst visibility initiative you've seen? Dialing back to the start of the project, what factors predicted the project outcome the most successfully?

     [Response from Peter Karel]   It was an oil and gas company, with the idea to implement RFID in a developing country. The project never really kicked off because the understanding of local business processes was missing and the local management was not committed to support the project. Ultimately, there was no understanding of the local process and how to get control of it prior to implementing visibility. We need to know what makes a process successful, vulnerable, or at risk prior to tackling the visibility initiative. Basically it's about knowing the problem before proposing a solution.

7.   [Question from Jonah McIntire]   Supply chain managers tend to acquire supply chain visibility through in-house development, off-the-shelf software, SaaS software, or as a perk from logistics service providers.

     a)   [Question from Jonah McIntire]   How would you suggest practitioners select the most appropriate method for themselves?

[Response from Peter Karel]   Fundamentally I trust this is first of all a question of core competence. You should be aware of whether the visibility is an integral component of your business. Take Dell for example, they grew and competed through a direct-to-consumer offering and part of that service was visibility to the build-up of a customer's specific order. For other companies who are following a make-to stock, deliver-from stock, this kind of visibility is not necessarily needed. At the end, if visibility is a core aspect of your business it should be held in house. If visibility is not mission-critical or a competitive differentiator, it should be acquired from outside.

For the acquiring process, create an RFQ or RFI and send it to the potential providers. Bring in the most promising responders and have them present the solution on-site, hopefully built on your own data and with a hands-on demonstration. The more structured this can be, the better the results. In addition, I would reach out to industry peers and get their direct feedback. This could be at conferences, through roundtables at professional membership organization, etc.

b)   [Question from Jonah McIntire]   Which of these is the rising star, and which is them is giving up market share?

[Response from Peter Karel]   The core competence of an LSP is to provide operational excellence in supply chain movements including the required visibility. Even though the IT gap is still significant, i.e. what shippers are expecting and what LSPs are offering (see 3PL Study), I believe long-term 3PLs will be more integrated in those processes as the industry is trying to close the gaps and in addition are moving in more supply chain related domains.

8.   [Question from Jonah McIntire]   Is supply chain visibility fundamentally a technology topic?

[Response from Peter Karel]   No, it's inherently a process where technology is important but not all encompassing. You must first understand your own business goals and processes, and then use technology tools to facilitate those processes. For me, the IT is an enabler of those processes. If you look at the 2013 3PL study from Cap Gemini and Panalpina, the "IT Gap" is the largest negative break between the 3PLs and their customers. Shippers consistently want more advanced or effective supply chain IT and particularly visibility from their LSPs.

9.   [Question from Jonah McIntire]   What are some of the most critical technology trends which you see converging on supply chain visibility? Why will these be critical areas to watch?

[Response from Peter Karel]   The mobile and cloud computing areas have a potential if we can overcome problems around security. The availability of data and services should certainly change the entire supply chain.

Fenwick, Scott (Director of Product Strategy at Manhattan Associates). 2013. Supply Chain Visibility. Interviewed by Jonah McIntire [via telephone with subsequent text review] Basel, CH on 25 February 2013. Transcript follows:

1.   [Question from Jonah McIntire]   How does your company come to the supply chain visibility topic? What major work are you doing or have done in this field?

[Response from Scott Fenwick]   Our approach is to separate the concept of supply chain visibility from the software solution, essentially creating a critical piece of technology infrastructure that provides visibility as a service to the rest of the enterprise. We have various software solutions which rely on visibility and also provide feeds in to it. So we separate visibility and event management from the core solutions. We suggest that the inability to separate these would be limiting, because no single operating aspects will provide visibility itself. In our approach, the platform delivers visibility as a side aspect of the main solutions. We do have the autonomy to offer a supply chain visibility software solution by itself, but we have found that the majority of successful visibility projects stem from a larger supply chain execution challenge. For example, that visibility is critically tied to DC execution, demand management, transport management, and so forth. This might be because it's hard to put an ROI on visibility. For years, CIOs rank visibility as an area of interest but tend to get cut from the list of funded projects because it is challenging to identify the ROI for a standalone visibility project. In today's world of the empowered customer, the need for visibility is a critical step to bring your supply chain closer to your end customer and therefore create the unwavering loyalty every business wants.

2.   [Question from Jonah McIntire]   You step in to an elevator with the new CEO of your company, and she asks you what supply chain visibility is about. How do you define it before the elevator doors open?

[Response from Scott Fenwick]   This is a tougher question. Supply chain visibility means so many things depending on the context of the conversation or who you are talking to. But supply chain visibility is about making sure the business has the awareness and insights needed to best run their business in the context of movement of goods.

3.   [Question from Jonah McIntire] What gets mixed up into the supply chain visibility which you feel should be left out? How do practitioners sharpen the blurry lines on the subject?

[Response from Scott Fenwick]   The thing that tends to blur the lines the most is EDI. A lot of people consider EDI their visibility tool. Five years ago this was a good starting point, but it's not the solution that is needed today. For the customers that were the most successful they have broken down the technical barriers and look past the "how do I get the data" such as EDI messages and instead focus on the end result and what business processes are being driven, and then backing into how you will get the data needed. We've seen the industry slowly shift from "where is my stuff" problem, to a "what is my cost picture." The insight that comes from visibility allows the business to react to their challenges and the cost picture which emerges. It's not just about orders and shipments against those orders. There are still a handful of customers who define visibility as a map with a ship icon on it and a list of stuff on that shipment. But that is really just step one out of many. But again, this is evolution of the process because it depends on the sophistication of the customer.

4.   [Question from Jonah McIntire]   Are there fundamentally different kinds of visibility or just different implementation approaches to achieving the same goal?

[Response from Scott Fenwick]   I think there are key and fundamental differences which have to be considered. There is visibility into process, into materials, and into business outcomes like cost and client satisfaction impact. Each of those has a different business drive and ultimately a different ROI theme. Of course, all these should be able to be brought back to a global picture of the supply chain and its place in the company. Whatever the individual visibility event, the supply chain managers should be able tie one element back to all the related supply chain processes and then to the business needs or performance. From a solution perspective, and especially as a software provider's perspective, the different types of visibility must ultimately tie back together.

5.   [Question from Jonah McIntire]   What was the best or worst visibility initiative you've seen? Dialing back to the start of the project, what factors predicted the project outcome the most successfully?

[Response from Scott Fenwick]   In one case we worked with a multibillion dollar retailer based in the USA. In their case they wanted to replace a homegrown legacy infrastructure which could not be grown at the pace of the business model. So there was a fixed scope. They also knew the exact capabilities of their current process and technology touch points, and what the gaps were for the desired solution. So the client began at a very mature level, with a clear plan of how the visibility would be phased in. In this case they were going to provide visibility inbound to their DCs and then outbound to their stores. They had a clear and organized approach to which benefits would be brought online at each point in time and which partners would need to be included and what data would be covered.

The second was in specialty apparel and manufacturing. The visibility was focused on inbound, around inventory and fulfillment. They were a success because they started with a very manageable chunk of work. After they achieved this scope, they learned their own risk exposures, which turned out to be further back in the supply chain. So in a second phase they extended backwards towards earlier manufacturing processes such as material selection and cutting, color dying sets, etc. Their success really derived from the fixed and reasonable scope and then the ability to work from that success and new information to identify a next-phase target.

6.   [Question from Jonah McIntire]   Supply chain managers tend to acquire supply chain visibility through in-house development, off-the-shelf software, SaaS software, or as a perk from logistics service providers.

a)   [Question from Jonah McIntire] How would you suggest practitioners select the most appropriate method for themselves?

[Response from Scott Fenwick] They need to think about their business from a growth perspective, in particular when comparing SaaS vs. COTS. Smaller businesses see a great allure towards SaaS options because the spend will be lighter, the risk is lighter, and the startup phase will be faster. But as the company grows there are often challenges. These may be around costs, which will become more expensive than fixed-cost options, or around handling more complex needs.

The challenge with using an LSP's visibility as a perk of being a client is a different issue. If your needs are around "where is the product while it's in transit," LSPs may be appropriate. But for more complex needs the LSPs alone are not enough and you end up trying to patch together many systems and providers.

Comparing COTS and in-house development, I think the only time this makes sense is when you have a very small business or challenge and when the ROI picture is not the primary consideration. What happens in most cases is that as the business users get some clarity and functions, they pull more and more scope out of the capabilities of the internal development teams. In many situations, private development is actually being mixed with a COTS solution in order to reach the niche or specific functions the company needs.

Certainly for any software acquisition, buyers should also be looking at questions around viability and continuity. As a CIO looking for a visibility package, the requirements around security and compliance are growing year over year and this is something that specific certifications can be used to vet providers. These are still benefits to a COTS solution.

7.   [Question from Jonah McIntire] How would you rate visibility impacting these areas of a typical business?

[Response from Scott Fenwick] We certainly (as an industry) started by focusing on inventory and focused on smoothing it out in order to have a quantifiable benefit. Outside inventory, the next area would be client satisfaction. Often this means that when I make a promise to a customer, the visibility helps assure that promise can be fulfilled. This is critical given that disappointing a customer almost always has lasting impacts.

8.   [Question from Jonah McIntire]   Is supply chain visibility fundamentally a technology topic?

[Response from Scott Fenwick]   I think it should be owned by the business, it's not a fundamentally technology topic. As a business topic it focuses us on the business case around ROI and process engineering. I think it becomes owned by the technology organization in the client company, simply because it's such a challenging integration problem which requires strong technical engineering. But ultimately if the business doesn't feel they own the topic and the solution, they either ignore it (therefore waste the capital) or they may actively try to work around it.

9.   [Question from Jonah McIntire]   Can you think of a technology change since 2000 which caused serious delay or advancement to supply chain visibility?

[Response from Scott Fenwick]   A few interesting ones for me are RFID and SaaS.

RFID may not be top of mind for supply chain visibility tools, but it's simply another way to get a lock on where goods are at. Active RFID has been particularly interesting in the cold chain logistics field. Unfortunately, it hasn't yet broken through barriers to adoption and become everything it can be.

Also, the SaaS based (or cloud based) deployments. These may be transactional functions like bookings or order offering. But for many businesses the SaaS deployment has a great potential for certain types of business problems.

10.   [Question from Jonah McIntire]   What are some of the most critical technology trends which you see converging on supply chain visibility? Why will these be critical areas to watch?

[Response from Scott Fenwick]   As more and more organizations mature in their ability to track materials, watching how mobile and GPS technology are brought into this domain will be interesting. Currently the focus around GPS is on assets, which tend to be expensive and reused and large (such as trucks). But coming out of major disasters like recent hurricanes, US retailers are looking for deeper integration of GPS into their inventory visibility. This can be used to drive things like compliance on processes, customer satisfaction, inventory disposition, and many other areas. This is an example of a broadly available technology which can be and is going to be brought to bear on the supply chain.

Wilcox, Shanton (Principal at Cap Gemini Consulting). 2013. Supply Chain Visibility. Interviewed by Jonah McIntire [via telephone with subsequent text review] Basel, CH on 1 February 2013. Transcript follows:

1.   [Question from Jonah McIntire]   How does your company come to the supply chain visibility topic? What major work are you doing or have done in this field?

      [Response from Shanton Wilcox]   We are a management consulting firm, in that we advise our clients on key topics relative to their operations and their objectives. In the context of a logistics strategy, we help put together their partner and extended network strategy in line with their objectives.

2.   [Question from Jonah McIntire]   You step into an elevator with the new CEO of your company, and she asks you what supply chain visibility is about. How do you define it before the elevator doors open?

      [Response from Shanton Wilcox]   It is the access to global information on supply chain operations. That may be a high level statement, but its everything from what is happening in the partner or extended network (PO transactional views), to the near real-time of physical movements within the supply chain.

3.   [Question from Jonah McIntire]   What gets mixed up in to the supply chain visibility which you feel should be left out? How do practitioners sharpen the blurry lines on the subject?

      [Response from Shanton Wilcox]   People tend to get latched on to their personal definition of supply chain visibility, and they have trouble accepting other definitions. People tend to be hardwired on this subject.

4.   [Question from Jonah McIntire]   Are there fundamentally different kinds
      of visibility or just different implementation approaches to achieving the
      same goal?

      [Response from Shanton Wilcox]   The nature of consulting is seeing
      across regions and across industries. It's all relative to the individual's
      concept. A luxury retailer may operate on a global basis, producing in
      South-East Asia and selling around the world. In other situations with
      local white-goods may be very extremely regional.

5.   [Question from Jonah McIntire]   How did you first get involved with
      supply chain visibility (either as an individual or a company)?

      [Response from Shanton Wilcox]   I've been in consulting for quite
      a while. Two projects back to back occurred in 2000. One was for a
      very large OEM manufacturer in the automotive industry. They faced
      coordination and synchronization of five tiers of supply flow, and
      driving efficiency. The second was a production supply chain for the
      largest defense contract in the world, a global supply chain producing
      major components, flowing into sub-assemblies, and then flowed out as
      aviation sections. The visibility to the components was critical because
      everything was fine tuned to ensure all pieces are serialized to a single
      aircraft.

6.   [Question from Jonah McIntire]   The management field is famous for
      fixating on topics and then discarding them a few years later. Do you
      think supply chain visibility is such a case? Is it a tool that is overhyped
      or undervalued?

      [Response from Shanton Wilcox]   I think it's still undervalued. Within
      the supply chain disruption topic, visibility is an example of a sub-topic
      that is being elevated. As supply chains spread out globally, the visibility
      is a core capability needed to manage these supply chains. Before, it was
      a capacity which helped differentiate a player. Today there are too many
      moving parts and they need to be managed on an exception basis.

7.   [Question from Jonah McIntire]   Supply chain managers tend to acquire
      supply chain visibility through in-house development, off-the-shelf
      software, SaaS software, or as a perk from logistics service providers.

a)   [Question from Jonah McIntire] How would you suggest practitioners select the most appropriate method for themselves?

[Response from Shanton Wilcox]   Going a step further back, we need to ask "what are the capabilities the company feels are their core value adding activities." This helps decides what parts are best handled by partners or providers. For example, do you want to own and operate the flow of these critical data elements, such as the flow of capital and the exact point at which ownership of goods has transferred? Am I going to hire the team, develop the enabling technology, or is simply the cost of doing global business. The context of the question is key. More often than not, the most appropriate are going to be off the shelf software, SaaS, or a perk from a provider. SaaS in particular has made visibility a realistic possibility. Building the partner network, the master data, the maintenance, etc., is arduous. In those cloud environments you are able to add incrementally, meaning that you often don't have to rollout to all suppliers at once because many are already on the platform. It is a true networks effect, i.e. Facebook, type business.

b)   [Question from Jonah McIntire]   Are there significant regional or industry variations which you've noticed?

[Response from Shanton Wilcox]   I don't see this as directed by the industry or region, but by the particular company.

8.   [Question from Jonah McIntire]   What are the business drivers for good visibility initiatives?

[Response from Shanton Wilcox]   The impetus out of the gate is when the company is in the fire-fighting mode, trying to track and keep up with manually tracking fulfillment. Therefore they are having stock outs, missing launch dates, and they are losing market share. They are realizing that throwing more bodies at the operational problem is not the answer, but they may not know what the answer will be.

9.   [Question from Jonah McIntire] How would you rate visibility impacting these areas of a typical business:

[Response from Shanton Wilcox]   If done correctly, it's around revenue and margin enrichment. For example for retailers I'm managing in store dates and stock out risk, I can rebalance inventory across the network based on how demand is materializing. But a more typical response might be "inventory and costs." The inventory comes down through overall visibility and there is less transport expediting. The more mature companies are looking at using visibility to help link forecast of short-season or short-lifecycle products over to the actual demand pattern, in an effort to maximizing margin by matching supply and demand. Think of how many companies are multichannel and the need for distributed order management, and now if I can see say four order streams from these channels I can allocate inventory to align inventory with orders and maximize margin.

10. [Question from Jonah McIntire]   If you were assembling a task force on supply chain visibility in your organization, what are the key skills or competencies you'd want to see in the staff selected to lead the project?

[Response from Shanton Wilcox]   People with an understanding of the operations you are trying to address. In retail, this may be store operations and inventory disposition. It may include logistics and warehouse, and also procurement and sourcing. This goes further back in the supply chain. And also finance, because these solutions are driving better operations information and looking at it on a global basis moves us away from letters of credits and towards open accounts, inventory on the books, stock age, etc.

11. [Question from Jonah McIntire]   What kind of timelines do you consider normal for a successful visibility project? How far apart are milestones like project proposal, approval, kick-off, go-live, and pay-back?

[Response from Shanton Wilcox]   I would approach it differently. I would ask, "how can we scope the initial launch so that we get true value and it does in fact work, and launch within 4–6 months." In many ways, this is needed to get leadership over the conceptual phase and to show results. It also shows that this will not be easy or perfect, but it controls risk and avoids an "all-or-nothing" decision.

12. [Question from Jonah McIntire]   Is supply chain visibility fundamentally a technology topic?

[Response from Shanton Wilcox]   No, it should never be technology. lead. It's not a technology topic. Technology enables the business solution. For example, the advancement of SaaS solutions plays a big role and allows more companies to access it. But if the underlying process is wrong, a technology applied to it will just accelerate the weaknesses. To the question of "can we do this without advanced technology?," it depends on the complexity or maturity. On some scales it's possible to use shared services and manual methods. But as the nature of the problem becomes more complex, like other business problems, technology provides a better solution. I advise all my clients: don't select a technology and then define the process, design the process and then employ a technology to facilitate it.

13.   [Question from Jonah McIntire]   Can you think of a technology change since 2000 which caused serious delay or advancement to supply chain visibility?

[Response from Shanton Wilcox]   Fundamentally it is the "cloud" or SaaS. Everything prior to "cloud" was point-to-point. In most cases it was also EDI, and hitting systems which were running on batch cycle times. The least sexy part of this topic is the data standardization, where we may have two definitions but agree to use a common one. Right now the data harmonization is driven by the cloud providers, because they have the most need to drive this in order to deliver value. It's part of their underlying base capabilities, to ensure everyone is talking about the same thing. There is also the efficiency of implementation of connecting to cloud vs. onboarding 800 suppliers on a one-by-one rollout.

14.   [Question from Jonah McIntire]   What are some of the most critical technology trends which you see converging on supply chain visibility? Why will these be critical areas to watch?

[Response from Shanton Wilcox]   We're still a long way away from maximizing the cloud. There may be some big names, but often they are in adjacent industries. Some industry or regions may be close to saturation, but most areas are just not maxed out at all. The global basis is missing.

Business intelligence will be key, because if you can embrace visibility and then clear out a lot of the noise by managing to exceptions, you are still collecting a core data set of huge volumes of transactions. Now how can you mine this to better inform your decision making? But business intelligence sits on a different time scale than supply chain visibility. BI currently plays a larger role in planning, whereas supply chain visibility is primarily focused on operations. BI is looking at past data in order to project into the future. They partner together well, and companies that realize that and take advantage of it can go to the next level.

15. [Question from Jonah McIntire]   Supply chains are cross-organizational, but specific investments in technology, training, and coordination need to be made for supply chain visibility. Do you see examples of these things being shared among the supply chain partners, or are they typically owned and managed by one party?

[Response from Shanton Wilcox]   At this point, it is still a situation where you have a significant player in the supply chain that is at a certain maturity or sophistication and they can't control their operations anymore and they are forced into making an investment to achieve supply chain visibility. I haven't seen a situation where two peers come together at the same moment to jointly start a project.

With cloud technology this may be changing, because it is less invasive. It offers a potential for asynchronous onboarding of players in a supply chain.

16. [Question from Jonah McIntire]   An IBM Chief Supply Chain Officer survey came back with interesting results in 2009. It showed that 70 percent of Chief Supply Chain Officers considered supply chain visibility a top challenge, but not a top priority. The top reasons provided by the respondents were: organizational silos, the fact they were not rewarded for visibility improvements, and the lack of effective tools. It's been three years now, how do you feel about this outlook? Has it changed and in what ways?

[Response from Shanton Wilcox]   I think when the survey was done, the macroeconomic picture makes this understandable. The supply chain executive was being squeezed hard on the fiscal side, making this not a high priority. But I think the outlook has changed in the last three years. The efficiency of the cloud-based solutions, and the resulting business environment which has emerged since 2009: I'm now doing business in more places in the world, but under pressure managing working capital. As visibility switches from a capital expense over to an operating expense, through the cloud, the priority of the topic will have risen.

Appendix B

The Supply Chain Visibility Scorecard Evaluation Instrument

Supply Chain Visibility Scorecard

How to Use the Scorecard:

1) For each visibility solution options, create one of these scorecards.
2) Add the list of business decisions which should be improved by supply chain visibility to the first column on the left.
3) After studying the solution design, and using the score guidelines provided, give each business decision a score for each metric.
4) Sum the scores by business decision and divide the sum by 24. This is the "fit %" for the solution as compared to the needs of the business decision, it is added to the column on the far right.
5) Average the fit percentages and add to the sheet the expected solution costs.
6) Plot the relationship between fitness percentage and solution costs and then eliminate any options which are strongly dominated.
7) The remaining options represent the frontier of tradeoffs between fitness and solution cost. Differentiating between these options requires assessing the organizations priorities.

NOTE: the scoring guide can be changed to provide more or less weight on certain metrics, as long as the same scoreguidelines are used by all evaluators and for all solution options.

Figure A.1   Page 1 of 3 of an example supply chain visibility scorecard instrument

Supply Chain Visibility Scorecard

Sensitivity

Score	Description
0	No data is captured to support the target business decision
1	Some relevant data is captured, but is incomplete
2	All data is captured but the accuracy of the data is unknown or known to be low
3	Data is complete and consistently biased (i.e. low quality but predictable)
4	All data needed to support the decision is captured, complete, consistent, and measurably high in accuracy.

Accessibility

Score	Description
0	Data remains in the capturing systems with no attempt to integrate the data for later use
1	Data remains in the capturing systems, but processes allow them to be manually integrated for ad-hoc tasks
2	The solution integrates all the decision-relevant data, but not all of it is retrievable by decision makers.
3	Data is integrated and available to the decision maker, but not using the methods they prefer.
4	All relevant data is integrated and accessible by any relevant path the decision maker could use.
5	All relevant data is integrated, accessible, and the approach to integrating data is easily adapted
6	All relevant data is integrated, accessible, and the integration approach is self-updating when confronting new data types or sources

Intelligence

Score	Description
0	There is no automated recognition from the solution that a business decision is needed
1	Sometimes there is recognition from the solution that a business decision is needed
2	The solution always knows that the business decision is needed
3	The solution's approach to recognizing the need for a business decision is easily updated by users
4	The solution's approach to recognizing the need for a business decision is self-updating

Decision-Relevance

Score	Description
0	The solution has no explicit input to this business decision.
1	The solution is a required information source for the decision maker. A user decides how and when to make the decision.
2	The solution is a required information source for the decision maker. The solution decides when the decision is taken and the user decides everything else
3	The solution offers a set of action alternatives based on the event; or
4	Narrows the selection down to a few; or
5	Suggests one action; and
6	Executes that suggestion if the human approves; or
7	Allows the human a restricted time to veto before automatic execution; or
8	Executes automatically, then necessarily informs humans; or
9	Informs the human only if asked; or
10	The solution decides everything and acts autonomously, with no notice given to the users

Figure A.2   Page 2 of 3 of an example supply chain visibility scorecard instrument

Supply Chain Visibility Scorecard

Visibility Solution Name: _____

Business Decision	Sensitivity	Accessibility	Intelligence	Decision-Relevance	Fit %

Estimated Total Cost: _____   Overall Fit %: _____

Figure A.3   Page 3 of 3 of an example supply chain visibility scorecard instrument

Works Cited

Aberdeen Group, 2007. *A View from Above: Global Supply Chain Visibility in a World Gone Flat* [White paper, online]. Available at: http://www.hk-dttn.com/portal08/html/Global-supply-visibility.pdf [accessed 1 April 2013].

Aberdeen Group, 2012. *Supply Chain Visibility Excellence: Mastering Complexity and Landed Cost* [White paper, online]. Available at: http://www.feg.unesp.br/dpd/cegp/2012/LOG/Material%20Complementar/Textos%20gerais/supply-chain-visibility%201.pdf [accessed 1 April 2013].

Adielsson, F., and Gustavsson, E., 2010. *Applying Supply Chain Visibility*. Master's Degree Thesis. Lund, Sweden: Lund Institute of Technology. Available at: http://lup.lub.lu.se/luur/download?func=downloadFile&recordOId=1835003&fileOId=1835020 [accessed 1 April 2013].

Albani, A., Müssigmann, N., and Zaha, J., 2007. A reference model for strategic supply network development. In: Fettke, P., and Loos, P., ed. 2006. *Reference Modeling for Business Systems Analysis* [Online]. Available at: http://intranet.iwi.unisg.ch/org/iwi/iwi_pub.nsf/wwwAuthorPublGer/BBC49340FFF2D03FC125771400786FE2/$file/30928.pdf [accessed 1 April 2013].

Anderson, C., 2013. *The Makers Revolution*, The Long Now Speakers Series, February 2013 [Podcast, online]. Available at: http://longnow.org/seminars/02013/feb/19/makers-revolution/ [accessed 1 April 2013].

Ashton, K., 2009. *The 'Internet of Things' Thing* [Editorial, online]. Available at: http://www.rfidjournal.com/articles/view?4986 [accessed 1 April 2013].

Auramo, J., 2006. *Implications of Supply Chain Visibility: Benefits in Transaction Execution and Resource Network Management*. Doctoral Thesis. Espoo, Finland: Helsinki University of Technology.

Baig, V., and Khan, T., 2001. Supply chain management: Value chain and value network logics. *Biennial Supply Chain Management Conference: "Opportunities and Challenges in Services Supply Chain"* [Online]. Available at: http://www.iimb.ernet.in/docs/scmc-papers/Viqar%20Ali%20Baig.pdf [accessed 1 April 2013].

Balakrishnan, A., Kumara, S., and Sundaresan, S., 1999. Manufacturing in the digital age: Exploiting information technologies for product realization. *Information Systems Frontiers*, vol. 1, no. 1, 25–50.

Barlow, A., and Li, F., 2004. Online value network linkages: Integration, information sharing and flexibility. *Electronic Commerce Research and Applications* [Online]. Available at: http://www.sciencedirect.com/science/article/pii/S1567422304000419 [accessed 1 April 2013].

Barratt, M., and Oke, A., 2007. Antecedents of supply chain visibility in retail supply chains: A resource based theory perspective. *Journal of Operations Management* [Online]. Available at: http://www.sciencedirect.com/science/article/pii/S0272696307000046 [accessed 1 April 2013].

Bierman, G., Buneman, P., and Gardner, P., 2003. *Ubiquitous Data* [White paper, online]. Available at: http://research.microsoft.com/en-us/um/people/gmb/papers/ubinet03.pdf [accessed 1 April 2013].

Bytheway, A., 1995. *Information in the Supply Chain: Measuring Supply Chain Performance* [Working paper, online]. Available at: http://dspace.lib.cranfield.ac.uk/handle/1826/1175 [accessed 1 April 2013].

Cap Gemini, 2012. *Supply Chain Visibility: Insight in Software Solutions* [White paper, online]. Available at: http://www.capgemini.com/resources/supply-chain-visibility-insight-in-software-solutions html [accessed 1 April 2013].

Carr, N., 2003. IT doesn't matter. *Harvard Business Review* [Online]. Available at: http://hbr.org/2003/05/it-doesnt-matter/ar/1 [accessed 1 April 2013].

Closs, D., Goldsby, T., and Clinton, S., 1997. Information technology influences on world class logistics capability. *International Journal of Physical Distribution & Logistics Management*, vol. 27, no. 1, 4–17.

Cooper, W., 2006. Textile and apparel supply chain management technology adoption: The Burlington industries case and beyond. *The Journal of Textile and Apparel Management* [Online]. Available at: http://www.tx.ncsu.edu/jtatm/volume5issue2/articles/Cooper/Cooper_Full_189-06.pdf [accessed 1 April 2013].

De Wit, B. and Meyer, R., 2005. *Strategic Synthesis*. Second Edition. Italy: Thomson.

Dudley, L. and Lasserre, P., 1989. Information as a substitute for inventories. *European Economic Review*, vol. 33, no. 1, 67–88.

Fawcett, S., Osterhaus, P., Magnan, G., Brau, J. and McCarter, M., 2007. Information sharing and supply chain performance: The role of connectivity and willingness. *Supply Chain Management: An International Journal*, vol. 12, no. 5, 358–68.

Goh, M., De Souza, R., Zhang, A., He, W. and Tan, P., 2009. Supply chain visibility: A decision making perspective. *IEEE* [Online]. Available at: http://

ieeexplore.ieee.org/xpl/login.jsp?tp=&arnumber=5138666&url=http%3A
%2F%2Fieeexplore.ieee.org%2Fiel5%2F5089335%2F5138149%2F05138666.
pdf%3Farnumber%3D5138666 [accessed 1 April 2013].

Hill, C. and Scudder, G., 2001. The use of electronic data interchange for supply chain coordination in the food industry. *Journal of Operations Management* [Online]. Available at: http://elogistics.lhu.edu.tw/may/course/ logistics/914b/pdf/43.pdf [accessed 1 April 2013].

Hoffman, K. and Hellström, D., 2008. Connectivity in logistics and supply chain management: A framework. In *14th Logistics Research Network (LRN) Conference* [Online]. Available at: http://www.lunduniversity.lu.se/ o.o.i.s?id=12683&postid=1058635 [accessed 1 April 2013].

Houlihan, J., 1987. International supply chain management. *International Journal of Physical Distribution & Logistics Management* [Online]. Available at: http:// www.emeraldinsight.com/journals.htm?issn=0960-0035&volume=17&issue =2&articleid=1694439&ppvc=1&articletitle=International+Supply+Chain+M anagement [accessed 1 April 2013].

IBM, 2009. *The Smarter Supply Chain of the Future: Global Chief Supply Chain Officer Study* [Report, online]. Available at: http://www-935.ibm.com/services/us/ gbs/bus/html/gbs-csco-study.html [accessed 1 April 2013].

Johansson, J. and Melin, J., 2008. *Supply Chain Visibility: The Value of Information.* Masters Thesis. Stockholm: Royal Institute of Technology.

Joshi, Y., 2000. *Information Visibility and its Effect on Supply Chain Dynamics.* Masters Thesis. Cambridge, MA: Massachusetts Institute of Technology.

Lee, L., Padmanabhan, V. and Whang, S., 1997. The bullwhip effect in supply chains. *Sloan Management Review* [Online]. Available at: http://www.ie. bilkent.edu.tr/~ie571/lee%20et%20al%20(1997).pdf [accessed 1 April 2013].

Licklider, J., 1960. Man-computer symbiosis. *IRE Transactions on Human Factors in Electronics* [Online]. Available at: http://groups.csail.mit.edu/medg/people/ psz/Licklider.html [accessed 1 April 2013].

Mason, S., Ribera, P., Farris, J. and Kirk, R., 2003. Integrating the warehousing and transportation functions of the supply chain. *Transportation Research* [Online]. Available at: https://www.google.com/url?sa=t&rct=j&q=&esrc=s &source=web&cd=2&cad=rja&ved=0CC8QFjAB&url=http%3A%2F%2Fcit eseerx.ist.psu.edu%2Fviewdoc%2Fdownload%3Fdoi%3D10.1.1.19.3516%2 6rep%3Drep1%26type%3Dpdf&ei=gZSSUb2nLYP-4QSczICoBw&usg=AF QjCNGeBHxjudKY843Hsoago6keR56Nqw&bvm=bv.46340616,bs.1,d.bGE [accessed 1 April 2013].

Mathews, J. and Shulman, A., 1999. Links, ties and bonds: Learning and knowledge creation in changing rd&e organisations. *Organizational Learning: 3rd International Conference* [Online]. Available at: http://notes.lancs.ac.uk/

pub/ol3.nsf/769f60f1be6577ad85256499006b15a5/f846f02fe7f49f89802567670
051ef76/$FILE/Matthews.pdf [accessed 1 April 2013].

McAdam, R. and McCormack, D., 2001. Integrating business processes for global alignment and supply chain management. *Business Process Management Journal* [Online]. Available at: http://www.imamu.edu.sa/Scientific_selections/ abstracts/Abstract%20IT%20%202/Integrating%20business%20processes %20for%20global%20alignment%20and%20supply%20chain%20 management.pdf [accessed 1 April 2013].

McIntire, J., 2009. The hollow enterprise and supply chain visibility. *Supply Chain Visibility Blog*, 12 June [Blog, online]. Available at: http://www.supply-chain-visibility.com/the-hollow-enterprise-and-supply-chain-visibility/ [accessed 1 April 2013].

Montgomery, A., Holcomb, M. and Manrodt, K., 2002. *Visibility: Tactical Solutions, Strategic Implications*. Chicago, IL: Cap Gemini Ernst & Young.

Moore, K., 2011. The best way to innovation? An important lesson from India. *Forbes* [Online]. Available at: http://www.forbes.com/sites/ karlmoore/2011/05/24/the-best-way-to-innovation-an-important-lesson-from-india/ [accessed 1 April 2013].

Parasuraman, R., Sheridan, T. and Wickens, C., 2000. A model for types and levels of human interaction with automation. *Journal IEEE Transactions on Systems, Man, and Cybernetics, Part A: Systems and Humans* [Online]. Available at: http://archlab.gmu.edu/people/rparasur/Documents/ParasSherWick20 00.pdf [accessed 1 April 2013].

Picot, A., Reichwald, R. and Wigand, R.T. 2003. *The Boundless Enterprise: Information, Organization and Management*. 5th Edition. Wiesbaden: Gabler Verlag.

Prahald, C. and Hamel, G., 1990. The core competence of corporations. *Harvard Business Review* [Online]. Available at: http://hbr.org/1990/05/the-core-competence-of-the-corporation/ar/1 [accessed 1 April 2013].

Rayport, J. and Sviokla, J., 1995. Exploiting the virtual value chain. *Harvard Business Review* [Online]. Available at: http://hbr.org/1995/11/exploiting-the-virtual-value-chain/ar/ [accessed 1 April 2013].

Reyes, P., Raisinghani, M. and Singh, M., 2002. Global supply chain management in the telecommunications industry: The role of information technology in integration of supply chain entities. *Journal of Global Information Technology Management*, vol. 5, no. 2, 48–67.

Salo, J. and Karjaluoto, H., 2006. IT-enabled supply chain management. *Contemporary Management Research*, vol. 2, no. 1, 17–30.

Simchi-Levi, D., Kaminsky, P. and Simchi-Levi, E., 2003. *Designing and Managing the Supply Chain: Concepts, Strategies, and Case Studies*. New York: McGraw-Hill.

Småros, J., 2005. *Information Sharing and Collaborative Forecasting in Retail Supply*

Chains. Doctoral Thesis. Espoo, Finland: Helsinki University of Technology, Laboratory of Industrial Management.

Småros, J., Lahtonen, J., Appelqvist, P. and Holmström, J., 2005. The impact of increasing demand visibility on production and inventory control efficiency. *International Journal of Physical Distribution & Logistics Management* [Online]. Available at: http://lrg.tkk.fi/logistics/publications/impact_of_demand_visibility.pdf [accessed 1 April 2013].

Storey, J. and Emberson, C., 2001. *The Realities of Supply Chain Management* [Online]. Available at: http://www.open.ac.uk/business-school/files/business-school/file/publications/research/WP01_7.pdf [accessed 1 April 2013].

Supply Chain Council, 2010. *Supply Chain Operations Reference Model Version 10* [Online]. Available at: http://supply-chain.org/.

Supply Chain Visions, 2005. *Benchmarking the Perfect Order: A Comprehensive Analysis of the Perfect Order in the Retail Industry* [Online]. Available at: http://www.scvisions.com/Benchmarking_the_Perfect_Order_v3.pdf [accessed 1 April 2013].

Tan, E., 2011. What Harvard is learning from the Mumbai Dabbawalas. *The Edge* [Online]. Available at: http://www.theedgemalaysia.com/sports/181274-what-harvard-is-learning-from-the-mumbai-dabbawalas.html [accessed 1 April 2013].

Thompson, R., Manrodt, K., Holcomb, M., Allen, G., and Hoffman, R., 2000. *Logistics @ Internet Speed* [Industry report, online]. Available at: http://www.manrodt.com/transtrends/images/pdf/report2000.pdf [accessed 1 April 2013].

Zhao, M., Dröge, C. and Stank, T., 2001. The effects of logistics capabilities on firm performance customer-focused versus information-focused capabilities. *Journal of Business Logistics*, vol. 22, no. 2, 91–107.

Zhou, H., and Benton Jr., W., 2007. Supply chain practice and information sharing. *Journal of Operations Management*, vol. 25, no. 6, 1348–65.

Index